MAKING FREEDOM

THE STEVEN AND JANICE BROSE LECTURES
IN THE CIVIL WAR ERA
William A. Blair, editor

MAKING FREEDOM

The Underground Railroad and the Politics of Slavery

R. J. M. BLACKETT

The University of
North Carolina Press
CHAPEL HILL

Set in Minion and Bodoni Poster Compressed
Manufactured in the United States of America

The paper in this book meets the guidelines for permanence
and durability of the Committee on Production Guidelines for
Book Longevity of the Council on Library Resources.

The University of North Carolina Press has been
a member of the Green Press Initiative since 2003.

Library of Congress Cataloging-in-Publication Data
Blackett, R. J. M., 1943–
 Making freedom : the Underground Railroad and the
politics of slavery / R.J.M. Blackett.
     pages cm.— (The Steven and Janice Brose lectures
     in the Civil War era)
Includes bibliographical references and index.
 ISBN 978-1-4696-0877-8 (cloth : alk. paper)
 ISBN 978-1-4696-3610-8 (pbk. : alk. paper)
 ISBN 987-1-4696-0878-5 (e-book)
 1. Fugitive slaves—United States. 2. Fugitive slaves—Legal status,
laws, etc.—United States. 3. Underground Railroad. 4. United States.
Fugitive slave law (1850). 5. Slavery—Political aspects—United States—
History—19th century. 6. Slavery—United States—Legal status of
slaves in free states. 7. United States—Politics and government—
1815–1861. I. Title.
 E450.B59 2013
 973.7'115—dc23

                         2013009243

To Martin Crawford and Christine Turner,
  two old and dear friends

Contents

Preface

Many years ago, while working on a study of the role African Americans played in the transatlantic abolitionist movement, I ran across William and Ellen Craft, former slaves who were enormously popular with British audiences. Following up their story, I discovered that they had escaped from slavery in Macon, Georgia, over the 1848 Christmas holidays. Ellen, who looked white, dressed as an invalid slave master, and William accompanied her as her slave. Within four days they were being hidden by sympathizers in Pennsylvania, where they spent a few days before moving on to the relative safety of Boston. There they established a life for themselves, a life that was shattered when, in October 1850, two slave catchers from Macon appeared, seeking to return them to slavery. All the evidence suggests that their former owner had long known where they were yet chose to wait until the passage of the Fugitive Slave Law two weeks earlier provided additional license to retake them. Much more draconian that the earlier version, the 1850 law unleashed political passions that few anticipated. At public meetings throughout the North, people pledged to defy the law; others saw it as nothing more than a means to reaffirm a pledge made by the founding generation. The South looked on wearily, deeply skeptical of the North's willingness to enforce what many saw as the last best chance to keep the Union together. The law, for all intents and purposes, nationalized the political debate over slavery. As if to thumb their noses at the law, the enslaved continued to escape in increasing numbers. In so doing, they actively joined the debate over the future of slavery. In this volatile political climate, the Crafts, and many other fugitives, became symbols of defiance and a yearning to be free. The pledge by the Boston black community and white supporters to protect the Crafts at all costs, in defiance of the law, only added to the sense of political crisis. The slave catchers were threatened physically and followed wherever they went by crowds of African Americans. In a coordinated effort, they were simultaneously sued by white members of the local Vigilance Committee for violating a number of ordinances. It is not clear that these suits had any legal merit; they were simply another way to intimidate the two Georgians. In the end, fearful for their safety, they returned to Georgia empty-handed. Although the attempt to recapture the fugitives had been repelled, supporters of the Crafts thought it best for the couple to leave the country once the president had publicly pledged his commitment to enforce the law at all costs and to punish those who resisted. By the end of the year, the Crafts were on their way to England, where they remained until 1869 when they returned to a United States free from slavery.

About ten years ago I decided to try to make sense of the political turmoil that followed in the wake of the Fugitive Slave Law by looking at how communities on both sides of the slavery divide organized to either resist or support enforcement of the law, and how slaves either entered or influenced the debate over the future of slavery by the act of escaping. Wanting to be as comprehensive as I possibly could, I made the rather foolish decision to cover the area from Virginia and Maryland in the east to Missouri in the west and north through the Free States to Canada. Having collected a mountain of data, I struggled over how the materials should be presented. The kind invitation from William Blair, director of the George and Ann Richards Civil War Center at Penn State University, to give the annual Brose Lectures in March 2012 forced my hand. My marching orders from Blair were simple enough: reevaluate the Underground Railroad. To do so, I chose to follow the trail laid out by the case of the Crafts. It is the Crafts who fashioned and executed their escape. Once they arrived in Pennsylvania, they were protected by members of the UGRR network who sent them to Boston. The passage of the Fugitive Slave Law and their former master's attempt to retake them threatened to destroy their newly won freedom. They and their supporters chose to defy both their former owner and the law. Those who came to their aid considered the law morally indefensible, one that had to be resisted. Supporters of the law thought otherwise: it was the law of the land and as such had to be obeyed and enforced. Defiance of this law—or any other law for that matter—they insisted, would set the country on the road to anarchy. I have added another feature to the discussion of the UGRR, one that was not a part of the Crafts' case, namely, the efforts of slavery's opponents to undermine the system by going into the South and enticing slaves to escape. Taken together, these were the vital elements of the UGRR. This approach takes its cue from William Still, the driving force in the Philadelphia Vigilance Committee, who opened his monumental history of the movement in the city—*The Underground Rail Road*, published in 1872, a history replete with scores of fugitives who acted on their own—with an account of Seth Concklin, a white northerner who went south to bring out members of Still's family and who died for his pains. Slaveholders did what they could to protect themselves against such incursions. They may have felt under siege and hemmed in by the movement to destroy slavery, but we should never underestimate their ability to defend their interests and to stymie opponents. Escaping slavery and being involved in the UGRR was dangerous business.

My thanks to my old friend, Martin Crawford, who read and

commented on the original draft; to the surprisingly large audiences who turned out, even on an unusually warm Saturday afternoon in March in Central Pennsylvania, and prodded me with questions about my findings; to the many archivists and librarians who responded promptly to my enquiries for information on local events and the people who were involved; to the very helpful staff of the Inter-library loan office at Vanderbilt University, who had a knack for finding me what I needed; and finally to my research assistants, Renee Stowitzky, Alexandria Cartaya, and Paula Gajewski, who took time out from their summer breaks to accompany me to libraries and places not normally found on tourists' maps. During these trips we talked history, drank beer, and many times found gems of information we could not have anticipated. The final draft of the first chapter benefited from the comments of Ira Berlin and David Blight and questions from the audience at a session of the 2012 conference of the Organization of American Historians.

MAKING FREEDOM

Introduction

Over the last few years, there has been reawakened interest in the operations of the Underground Railroad (UGRR), an interest that has risen to levels not seen since the 1890s, when the children of those involved in aiding slaves escape sought to preserve (and some would say glorify) the memory of their parents and the work they did in what was, by any measure, the most clandestine aspect of the antebellum abolitionist movement. The new history is more dispassionate in its praise of the range and effectiveness of the efforts of those who participated in the movement. It has also widened its coverage to include many who, in the earlier histories, had been thought to have played little or only peripheral roles. But most important of all, the new studies assess the work of the slaves themselves in affecting their own freedom.[1] This new approach reflects a corresponding popular interest in the abolitionist movement. There are local, state, and federal government agencies devoted to promoting the study of the movement, websites that provide invaluable information on local events, countless conferences devoted to the theme, and national and local museums that explore the meaning of freedom and the workings of the UGRR. In fact, it is next to impossible nowadays to give a lecture on any aspect of the abolitionist movement without being asked a question about the UGRR.

This study takes its cue from these modern approaches to the movement by emphasizing what the enslaved did. It was the glorification of the work of northern abolitionists, mainly Quakers, in many of the early histories of the movement that led Larry Gara to question this approach and to point to the fact that the initiative to escape came almost exclusively from the enslaved themselves. Since then, other historians, such as Keith Griffler, have explored the many ways in which African American communities in Ohio were central to the activities of the movement in that state. What occurred in Ohio was replicated in many other areas of the North. It was these communities, particularly those in urban areas, that were the backbone of the movement. They provided havens for fleeing fugitives, transported them from one station to another, and, when necessary, dared the authorities to reclaim those seeking freedom. Furthermore, Stanley Harrold and Kate Clifford Larson have highlighted the fact that there were those who crossed into the South to entice and aid slaves to escape.

As in many of these studies, my focus is on the slaves as well as those who aided them where it mattered most: in the South. The movement can conveniently be divided into two separate but related areas of activity: what occurred at the point of escape and what happened once the escaping slave reached free territory. What the slaves and their helpers did, I hope to show, affected the politics of the areas and states from which they escaped. Understanding these points of departure leads to an appreciation of the many and complex ways the politics of scale affected conditions in these areas, from Missouri in the west to Maryland and Virginia in the east, the points of greatest friction between slavery and freedom. Put simply, when, for example, slaves escaped from Berlin, Worcester County, on the Eastern Shore of Maryland, their action had significant political ramifications locally, which in turn rippled outward into state politics and on many occasions further into national and international politics. The same is true of the response to efforts to reclaim the enslaved who had reached the relative security of northern communities. Admittedly, it is not always easy to trace a direct political line between Berlin and Annapolis, Maryland, and Washington, D.C., or for that matter West Chester and Harrisburg, Pennsylvania, and Washington, D.C., but it can be done.

At the heart of these political connections in the decade leading up to the Civil War lies the 1850 Fugitive Slave Law. It is not that slave escapes prior to 1850 did not produce political ripples, only that the law, part of the Compromise of 1850, by expressly making recapture and rendition of runaways a national issue—one that came to symbolize in the eyes of many in the South the willingness of the North to recognize the legitimacy of the South's right to hold slaves and to protect that property—set the stage on which the actions of slaves in Berlin, Maryland, were played out not only locally but also across the state line in West Chester, Pennsylvania, and sometimes in the nation's capital. The law not only stiffened the penalties imposed by the original Fugitive Slave Law of 1793; it also made it easier for slaveholders to reclaim slaves who had escaped to a free state. It insisted as well that citizens had to become involved in the recapture of slaves if requested to do so by the authorities. The residents of West Chester were transformed by the law into slave catchers. Once the law was adopted, one Maryland newspaper, employing customary hyperbole, reported that local slaveholders had already taken steps to recover many of the thousands of fugitives living in Columbia, Lancaster, Harrisburg, and Pittsburgh, Pennsylvania, and predicted "a great storm in that direction."[2] A storm there was, if not the sort anticipated by the editor. Widespread northern public condemnation of the law in the months following its adoption in September 1850, and the open declaration of resistance to its enforcement by black communities and their white allies in and out of state government, heightened rather than lessened sectional tensions. For many in the South and their political supporters in the North the enforcement of the law spoke to the willingness of the Free States to recommit themselves to the compromises over slavery that had done so much, they believed, to keep the nation whole. Opponents of slavery saw things differently and bridled at the willingness of the federal and many northern state governments and local authorities to concede to such demands. The law quickly came to encapsulate the larger debate over the future of slavery and by extension the nature of the union. Firing that debate, I suggest, were the actions of the slaves who found countless and ingenious ways to put distance between themselves and those who claimed them as property. In doing so, they had a profound if not always appreciated influence on the debate over slavery's future.

Unearthing local events requires the careful reading of countless local newspapers for the decade of the 1850s, a time when most newspapers, especially those in major cities, increasingly were becoming dailies. It is here that one comes to appreciate the degree to which slaves sought their freedom; here are to be found the many ways southern authorities tried to stymie these activities, to control all they considered a threat to the security of slave property. And here is to be found the passion and determination protectors of the system brought to its defense against those they considered subversives of good order. Definitions of "subversives" were rather elastic. They included northern legislators who found ways to undermine enforcement of the Fugitive Slave Law through the adoption of local ordinances; northern black communities and their white supporters who prevented slaveholders from reclaiming their lost property; southern whites who were supposedly corrupted by abolitionist propaganda and who chose to act on those beliefs; free blacks, who many suspected were close allies of the slaves and for that reason should be watched closely or, better yet, expelled or re-enslaved; and northern whites and African Americans who went into the South disguised as legitimate traders and schoolteachers, seamen and laborers, bent on enticing slaves to escape. Finally, it is here that one finds the accounts of the many ways local and state authorities marshaled the full weight of the courts and police forces to impose their will on anyone suspected of undermining the system.

As will become immediately apparent, this study relies heavily on the recounting and recapturing of events and the individuals who participated in them. It is one way, I believe, to bring to life the many political actors, especially the enslaved, who have largely been lost to history, and to come to grips with their perceptions of freedom and liberty. The first chapter opens with Henry Banks's decision to leave Virginia in 1853 and the efforts of his former master to retake him. The actions of Banks and others who followed a similar course tell us a great deal about the enslaved's notions of freedom. But it is important to keep in mind that while Banks was successful, many others failed to attain their goal, were recaptured and returned to slavery, were sold further south and permanently separated from family, or, worse yet, lost their lives in the effort to reach freedom. It is in these stories of danger and determination that we come to appreciate the commitment to freedom of those who were enslaved. Against this can be juxtaposed slaveholders' deep investment in what Leigh Fought aptly describes as "the privileges of property."[3] The second chapter explores the impact of a series of fugitive slave cases in southeastern Pennsylvania in the wake of the passage of the 1850 Fugitive Slave Law. It also explores the role of the area's black communities as they organized to defend the fugitives in their midst. Such actions exacerbated political tension in the state as well as increased conflict between Pennsylvania and the slaveholding states to the south. What happened in this area of Pennsylvania was played out in other sections of the North also. The final chapter takes a cue from William Still's compendium, *The Underground Railroad*, which opens not with a major slave break but with the death of Seth Concklin, a white northerner, who lost his life attempting to free the family of Still's brother

Peter from slavery in Alabama. It shifts our gaze to the activities of outsiders who went south to entice slaves to escape, the extent to which slaves planning to escape were aided by southern free blacks and fellow slaves, and the efforts of slaveholders and southern authorities to protect themselves against these subversives.

1. Making Their Way to Freedom

"I find myself in a Position to address you a few lines and I hope that they may find you in as good health as I am myself in." There is nothing unconventional about this opening salutation except that it was written by a slave to his master soon after he had escaped. It is unusual in another way: the author clearly meant to thumb his nose at his master, to demonstrate his capacity for independent action, and to make clear his desire for freedom. But this sort of communication, written so soon after an escape, ran the risk of destroying the best laid plans. That it did not says something about the individual who executed what was a masterful plan of escape from slavery in 1853. The letter was written by Henry W. Banks to William M. Buck, a forty-three-year-old slave master of Front Royal in the Shenandoah Valley of Virginia, and postmarked from New York City February 15, 1853. Banks, who was described by contemporaries as a mulatto, had been hired by Buck in 1849 from his owner, Edward W. Massey, who lived a short distance from Front Royal. Evidently, Banks had requested the move so he could be near his wife. But he may have had other plans. Less than two years after the transfer, Massey got word that Banks was planning to escape. Massey had him jailed, but Buck intervened and had him released, confident that the rumors were baseless. In April 1852, Massey got wind of another planned escape and this time sold Banks to a local slave trader. Again, Buck came to Banks's defense: family connections, he predicted confidently, would keep Banks close to home. To convince Massey that there was nothing to the rumor, Buck agreed to post a security of $800 should Banks escape before the expiration of the contract they had first signed in 1849 and renewed every year since. In less than a year, Banks was gone—where to no one knew. Massey was convinced he had fled with his brother Landon and despaired of ever retaking him. His "smartness," Massey predicted, was a "sure guarantee for his escape."

Two days after the escape, William Buck received his first letter from Banks, ostensibly from New York City. In it Banks spoke of plans to go to either Albany or Buffalo and, curiously, informed Buck of the escape route he had taken. First, he had gone north to Washington County, Maryland, a few miles short of the Pennsylvania line. But rather than cross into free territory at that point, he instead turned southeast to Baltimore, where he spent two days. From there, he headed north to Philadelphia, where he rested for one night before moving on to New York City. These details, it seems, were meant to throw off any likely pursuers. If Banks had escaped, as he states in his letter, on the 13th, then he could not have arrived in New York two days later, given the stops he says he had made on the way. But Buck was not fooled; he suspected Banks had gone directly to Philadelphia. In fact, he sent an advertisement announcing the escape to Kinzell and Doyle, slave traders in Clear Spring, Washington County, Maryland, in the hope they could cut Banks off before he reached free territory. Unfortunately for Buck, both were away on business in Pennsylvania at the time.

Among slaveholders at least, it was believed that Banks had not acted alone. Edward Massey suspected he had left in the company of his brother. While it is not clear that Banks had worked with others, there seemed to have been a number of other escapes from the area around the same time, suggesting a degree of collusion and planning among the slaves. Two weeks after Banks left the area, Thomas Ashby, William Buck's stepbrother, was in Philadelphia searching for a slave named George who had escaped about the same time Banks did. George had written a number of letters to family and friends back home from an address in Philadelphia that Ashby described as "one of the receptacles for fugitives and their correspondence." Ashby tracked him to the address from which the letters were written, but George had already moved on. He hired a policeman with fifteen years' experience tracking fugitives, but it was, as he told his brother, like "looking for a needle in a haystack" because there were so many places to hide and "such a variety of faces" that confuse and "throw difficulties in the way." Ashby even contacted Edward D. Ingraham, the city's commissioner responsible for hearing fugitive slave cases, showing him several of the letters George had written, but Ingraham had few answers to the riddle of George's whereabouts. In the end, Ashby gave up, suggesting to his brother that he should instead employ someone who knew both Banks and George and could commit to spending "several weeks" in the city.

Following his stepbrother's advice, William Buck contacted Henry H. Kline, a deputy marshal who almost two years earlier had been a member of the Philadelphia posse that accompanied Edward Gorsuch, a Maryland slaveholder, to Christiana, Pennsylvania, on his ill-fated attempt to reclaim three of his slaves. In spite of his experiences at Christiana, Kline seemed to have remained active in the business of tracking down fugitive slaves. Buck suggested Kline hire a policeman from each of the city's wards where African Americans lived to help him capture Banks and George. Unfortunately, Kline was away when Buck's letter arrived. When he finally replied in April, he declined to follow Buck's advice because, as he observed, many of the policemen were under the influence of abolitionists and were opposed to hunting down fugitives.

He also did not think it wise to write Banks a letter in the hope of ferreting him out because, as he informed Buck, blacks in the city protected fugitives and quickly moved them out once they got wind of any danger. Instead, he proposed to hire two or three men he could trust. He had a few leads, he added hopefully, from a "pigeon" who had informed him that Banks was not in the city at the moment but would soon return. This news must have raised Buck's spirits. If it did, they were soon dashed when Buck received a second letter from Banks in April, posted from a steamship on the Allegheny River in Pennsylvania, saying he had changed his plans and was now on his way to California. Buck shared this latest letter with Edward Massey, who responded that Banks was leading them on a merry dance. This most recent letter, Massey believed, was meant to throw Buck's "attention away from him." He knew Banks well enough to know that he was not on his way to California, nor would he settle on a farm or in a small town such as Aspinwall, Pennsylvania, along the Allegheny River, where a brother lived and where he would be most vulnerable, but would choose instead the security and anonymity provided by a large city such as Pittsburgh, Philadelphia, or New York. That is where they should concentrate their search. But Ashby's efforts in Philadelphia had drawn a blank, as had Kline's. Massey also suspected that Banks had the support of someone who knew the preferred way of reaching California and was feeding him this information.

Banks was also using stamps that were designed to throw Buck and Massey off his track: "He has found means," Massey observed, "to have a very imperfect stamp put on his letters." Not only was the stamp imperfect (whatever that means), but the letter was headed "steamship," without giving the name of the ship. Massey suggested that Buck contact the postmaster at Front Royal to verify that the stamps used by Banks were legitimate. Massey may have been skeptical about Banks's ultimate destination, but others who Buck had hired to help him recapture Banks were convinced he was headed to his brother's home in western Pennsylvania. The idea was not too far-fetched. If Banks was not heading to Aspinwall, then he may have been trying to make connections with Maria Cooper and her family, recently freed slaves from Front Royal who had settled in Washington County just south of Pittsburgh. In spite of his best efforts, Buck failed to locate Banks. The trail went cold until November 1853, when Buck received a third letter from Banks informing him that he had arrived safely in Hamilton, Ontario.[1]

While Banks's escape speaks to the fragility of the slave system, it does provide us with an opportunity to explore further the nature and consequences of what Henry Bibb, who had escaped from slavery in Kentucky, called the "work of self emancipation." At first glance it seems odd that Banks would go to such lengths to stay in touch with his former master. There is no doubt that he felt some attachment to the man who had protected him from the dark unknown of the internal slave trade. Banks even offered in his final letter from Canada to repay Buck the $800 security he had to forfeit when Banks left. But neither his attachment to his wife and friends in Front Royal nor the gratitude he felt for Buck's treatment of him diminished Banks's determination to be free. His chances of reaching freedom were increased if he could throw off his tracks any slave catchers Buck might send. His first two letters were meant to do just that. Edward Massey was convinced they were part of a carefully laid plan of deception contrived by a smart slave who for years had been planning to run.[2]

Both Buck and Massey suspected that free blacks in and around Front Royal had helped Banks escape by providing him with a pass. This seems unlikely; after all, Banks was literate and did not need the assistance of anyone to write him a pass. To the dismay of slaveholders, the pass, which was meant as a mechanism to control the movement of slaves and limit their chances of escape, had been transformed in the hands of slaves into a passport to freedom. Advertisements for runaways frequently made reference to the fact that fugitives could read and write, had written passes for themselves, or had acquired passes from others. We do not know the exact details of the poster Buck sent to Kinzell and Doyle, the slave traders operating out of Clear Spring, Maryland, but by the early 1850s advertisements made frequent reference to the fact that slaves were using their literary skills to effect their escape. When, for example, Prince, a twenty-five-year-old harness maker, escaped with five others from a "camp" in Athens in southeast Tennessee in September 1853, George Washington Reid informed readers of a Nashville newspaper that Prince had a map in his possession, that he could read and write, and that he was making his way to Illinois using a pass that Reid implied he had written himself. Three months later, John Patton, a fellow Tennessean, made public that a slave named Sam had escaped from Williamson County with free papers that were the property of David McLamore. The implication was that Sam had either stolen the papers or McLamore had given them to him to use in his escape to Illinois.[3] In March 1851, John Gilliam of Powhatan County, Virginia, advertised for two runaways, Marigold and William, who, he believed, had acquired what he described as "spurious passes" or forged free papers with the help of free blacks that they were using to move around freely and to find work on the canal near Lynchburg and on the railroad. An Orange County, North Carolina, slaveholder, John Glenn, suspected that his slave Jack was making his way through Virginia to a free state using "forged free papers or the pass of some free negro."[4]

The ease with which slaves moved about the rural South facilitated the transmission of news and pushed slave systems to enact laws to limit their mobility. The problem was exacerbated in urban areas, where slaves had even greater freedom to move around and to consort with fellow slaves and working-class whites. The situation in Nashville, Tennessee, was fairly typical. Periodically during the 1850s, the local authorities would make a concerted effort to clamp down on the movement of slaves in the city by fining those employers who broke the law prohibiting hiring slaves without written permission, and those whites and free blacks who "entertained" slaves or sold them alcohol. William Graham, for instance, was fined $10 plus costs for allowing a slave to sleep in an outhouse without permission, $2 and costs for permitting the same slave to hire his time, and an additional $20 and costs for, as one newspaper put it, "combining with the same slave to hire his own time."[5] Periodic police raids had no perceptible long-lasting effects on these connections. Similar connections existed in small towns and settlements throughout the South. In Maddenville, a crossroads close to Stevensburg in Culpeper County, Virginia, for example, a small tavern, general store, and inn owned by Willis Madden, a prosperous free black, provided a meeting place where whites, free blacks, and slaves could "play cards and drink." It was, Scott Christianson has written, an "important information clearing house for slaves as well. Many regarded it, like the courthouse and the plantation dining room, a gold mine of intelligence about what whites were up to." It is, Julius Scott argues, in these settings of "people on the move"—places where they congregated—that news of developments elsewhere were orally transmitted, where rumors were legend. When James Redpath, the radical journalist, toured the South in the late 1850s, he was stunned by the speed with which news traveled among slaves in spite of strict surveillance on the plantations and the existence of patrols, which, he observed, did little to stem the movement of slaves "over large tracts of the country." This system of "secret travel" had its origin, he reported, in the slaves' "love of gossip and wish to meet their friends and relatives." The more oppressive the system became, the quicker gossip was replaced by a deep yearning for freedom.[6] When William Andrew Jackson, Jefferson Davis's coachman, escaped from Richmond as Union forces gathered for a possible assault on the Confederate capital in 1862, Union commanders in Fredericksburg consulted him on the layout of the enemy's defenses. For years, Jackson had moved about the city with relative freedom, working as a messenger for a local bank before he was hired by Davis. When he later toured Britain to promote the cause of the Union, he added the sort of legitimacy to the cause that only someone with first hand information on the inner workings of the Confederacy could.[7]

But Henry Banks's letters to Front Royal point to another feature of the system of communication employed by slaves. Apparently either slaves or free blacks in Front Royal had gotten word to George and Banks by mail that slave catchers were on their heels. It frustrated Thomas Ashby's carefully laid plans to intercept the fugitives in Philadelphia. "It is most unfortunate," he wrote Buck, that "those letters fell into the hands they did. Could they have been intercepted without being known amongst the negroes, a correspondence kept up, purporting to be from either or all, his apprehension would have been without question. Now such a correspondence is out of the question for the reason I fear it is known in Front Royal that I came here for him." Clearly, Ashby was baffled by the ease with which letters were exchanged between the fugitives and their friends and family in Front Royal. Both he and Massey wondered if the local postmaster was colluding with slaves or if he was simply ignoring his responsibilities under local law to prevent the transmission of such letters. Massey put it bluntly to Buck: the local postmaster should be asked whether it was "best to deliver letters to slaves without informing their masters." He knew the answer, but that did little to ease his concerns.[8]

Slaves who had left the South used the postal service to communicate with loved ones and friends left behind. The Reverend Robert Ryland had to warn his congregation at the First African Church in Richmond, Virginia, against receiving letters from escaped former members of the church in which they described the best ways to reach freedom.[9] The use of the mail by abolitionists in the mid-1830s riled slaveholders, who called for prohibiting the dissemination of abolitionist materials by this means. By the 1850s improvements in the postal system and a reduction of rates dramatically lowered the cost of sending a letter. Starting in 1851, mail sent between New York and California, for example, was charged a flat rate of "3 cents per half ounce." This meant that anyone (and that included fugitive slaves such as Banks) could correspond with distant family and friends cheaply.[10]

The streams of communication flowed in both directions. Slaves contemplating escape sometimes made plans with friends and family in the North and Canada before leaving. John Bull and Joe Mayo, two of five runaways found on the steamship *Keziah* in the James River in 1858, knew where they were going. Bull had arranged with friends in Canada to be hired as a waiter in a local hotel. Mayo was off to New York City to meet his wife, who had escaped a few years earlier. Samuel Green had heard of Canada and the UGRR from Harriet Tubman during one of her trips to the Eastern Shore of Maryland to abduct slaves. Susan Brook, forty, fled Norfolk in April 1854, six months after her son had arrived in Canada. It was three years after Caroline Aldridge's brother escaped to Canada from Maryland in 1854 before she, at age twenty-three, decided to follow him.[11]

William Still of the Philadelphia Vigilance Committee received numerous requests from runaways in Canada asking him to contact family members left behind to arrange their departure. Samuel Miles, who took the name Robert King after he escaped from Somerset County, Maryland, in August 1855, wrote Still from St. Catherine, Canada, asking him to contact his wife Sarah, who was living in Baltimore, to let her know where he was and to encourage her to leave. Lewis Burrell escaped with his brother Peter from Alexandria, Virginia, in April 1856, leaving his wife Winna Ann and two children, Joseph and Mary, behind. After nearly three years in Canada, Burrell wrote Still, saying that he had found out his wife was then living in Baltimore and that she wanted to leave. But Burrell feared that a letter from Canada would alert both her master and local authorities. Instead, he suggested that Still write to Samuel Madden, a Baptist preacher—and the son of Willis Madden, whose tavern and inn at Maddenville, was a hub, as we have seen, of communication for slaves—who he knew would help. According to Christianson, Samuel Madden "occasionally returned to the area to visit his kin and hold illegal prayer meetings at Berry Hill and other local spots; he also exchanged letters and intelligence on behalf of runaways and their loved ones." In spite of warnings from Still, John Henry Hill wrote frequently to family and friends in Petersburg, Virginia, arranging for their escape. Hill, a twenty-six-year-old carpenter, had escaped from Richmond in January 1853. A slave in Petersburg, Hill was hired out, agreeing to pay his master, James Mitchell, $150 at the end of the hire in December 1852. Instead, Mitchell took Hill to Richmond where he planned to sell him. Hill put up a fierce fight when he was taken to an auction house and managed to escape. He was hidden by a friend of his mother for nine months before he could safely leave Richmond for Norfolk, where he boarded a ship for Philadelphia, leaving behind a wife who was free and two children. Over the next few years Hill kept up a constant stream of letters to Still with instructions and suggestions about the best way to get his family out. Hill's wife and children would later join him, as would his uncle Hezekiah, a sixty-three-year-old slave, in 1856 and his brother James in 1861.[12]

William Still was the conduit, the transmitter of communication, between Hill and his family in Virginia. He even arranged to have a large box of goods belonging to Hill's wife shipped out of Petersburg to Canada. Still also used a number of unnamed black and white contacts to carry letters between Hill and his family. Writing letters was risky and dangerous business; should they fall into the wrong hands, it could lead to the imprisonment of the courier or contact person and the selling of the runaway's spouse. It was the discovery of a letter from his son of the same name who had escaped to Canada earlier that raised suspicions among authorities in Cambridge, Maryland, that the Reverend Samuel Green was involved in the frequent escape of slaves from the area. Authorities in others parts of the South were similarly vigilant. In Louisville, for example, they built several cases against local opponents of slavery on letters they had received from the North and Canada. When the local police raided the home of John C. Long, a white dyer and scourer, who had helped a slave named Alfred to escape, they found a cigar box filled with letters from Westport and Chillicothe, Ohio, written by Long's brother, asking for a description of Alfred so he could write a free pass that would allow Alfred to travel to Canada. Another case in Louisville involved Rachel, twenty years old and the only slave of J. C. Wetherlee, who escaped to Chatham, Canada, in 1856 assisted by F. George Cope, a well-known white grocer. The evidence suggests that Rachel took in washing for Cope. But there was apparently more to the relationship. Rachel frequently visited Cope's shop and home and according to some witnesses spent an inordinate amount of time in Cope's room. Cope would later admit that she had become his "wife in Heaven." Cope and Rachel planned her escape with the understanding that, once the anxiety caused by her escape had abated, he would join her in Canada. But Cope may have been deceived, for when a month later Wetherlee went to Canada to persuade Rachel to return, she handed him Cope's letters. They would be used by Wetherlee in his suit against Cope for aiding in Rachel's escape. When the case came to trial in 1859, the jury deadlocked, according to one wag because there were too many "amalgamating and kidnapping difficulties." At a second trial ten months later, Cope was found not guilty, by which time he had languished in prison for two years.[13]

But if writing letters was risky business, it was a risk many were willing to take. The abolitionist, Laura Haviland, remembered frequent visits from former slaves who asked her to write letters to their family and friends using as conduits "white people who were their friends." On the coastal arm of the UGRR, black seamen carried letters between slaves and northern friends and family. Slaves still in bondage, David Cecelski has argued, had extensive contact with slaves who fled or free blacks who migrated to northern cities. Those involved in getting word to family and friends by letter sometimes used what Still called "Underground Railroad parables," but even this ruse proved unavailing at times.[14] The mere suspicion that a white person in the South was partial to the cause of the slave generally resulted in rough justice. The experiences of a white schoolteacher in Mississippi with the quaintly Dickensian name P. Smellee, was not atypical. Although Smellee was not involved in the UGRR, he was clearly partial to abolition. Not long after he was appointed principal of the Jackson public school in 1854, Smellee wrote a friend in the North but forgot to address the letter properly. The local postmaster opened the letter to see to whom it should be sent, read its content, and, when he discovered it contained "infamous Abolitionist sentiments," passed it on to the mayor. Smellee was dismissed and left town ahead of an irate mob.[15] Others were not so lucky.

But what prompted slaves such as Henry Banks to begin the "work of self emancipation"? My interest here is in those who left the South permanently. As John Hope Franklin and Loren Schweninger have shown, they comprised a small but nonetheless significant number of the many who fled. The politics of self-emancipation took different forms and were driven by different considerations—some opportunistic, others calculated. In interviews with William Still runaways revealed their reasons for seeking freedom. Thomas Madd, twenty-two, left Easton, Maryland, after being severely flogged for what he thought was a minor infraction. As in many other cases, Madd's owner had also threatened to sell him. A cruel flogging prompted Mary Epps, forty-five and the mother of fifteen children (four of whom had been sold away earlier), to leave in March 1855. She later paid $400 to get her husband Francis out, although the records are silent on what became of her children. In a system where the threat of family separation through sale was ever present, some slaves fled without their family, hoping to be reunited with them later. Nelson Harris, twenty-seven, escaped from Richmond in October 1853, leaving his wife and two children behind, because he was worried that he was about to be sold. When Jane Davis, a sixty-year-old mother of twelve, lost six of her children to the internal slave trade, she decided to flee from the Eastern Shore of Maryland. In these and other cases, escape became a way to reunite families. Peter Johnson escaped from Berlin, Worcester County, Maryland, to join his wife, who had left months before. In some cases where one spouse was free, escapes also led to the reuniting of families in freedom. Not long after John Judah escaped from Maryland in May 1855, his wife arrived in Philadelphia. Some runaways, such as Zechariah Mead, simply followed the example of others. He fled when fifteen of his mistress's twenty slaves decamped for the North.[16]

Slaves also fled when, in their minds, masters broke hiring and other agreements, unwritten labor contracts if you will. Hezekiah Hill, John Henry Hill's sixty-three-year-old uncle, had an agreement with his owner to buy his freedom, but his master reneged on the contract after Hill had paid almost $2,000. In 1855 Hill fled Petersburg for Richmond, where he was "hidden under a floor by a friend." A number of attempts to get him out by boat had to be abandoned as too dangerous. Finally, after thirteen months, Hill was put on board a steamer for Philadelphia with the seven-year-old son of the man who had hidden him, leaving behind his wife and two sons. He arrived in Toronto in January 1856. When masters arbitrarily changed the terms of hire, slaves invariably resisted. Both Charles King, a twenty-three-year-old ship carpenter who paid his master $10 per month, and Robert White, thirty-five, who paid $9, left Norfolk Virginia in September 1854, when their masters demanded increased payments. Lewis Francis, twenty-seven, arrived in Philadelphia in December 1855, after leaving Baltimore, where he had been hired out since a boy to a barber. Francis was allowed to keep $250 annually from his wages, paying his owner, a Mrs. Delinas of Harford County, Maryland, $8 a month. When Delinas became dissatisfied with the amount she was receiving and threatened to sell Francis if the amount was not increased, he left.[17]

Henry Banks's first letter is a curious mix of longing for the people and places he left behind and an expression of a firm determination to be free. Not only did he ask William Buck to pass on greetings to a number of friends and family, he also declared in no uncertain terms, "I never expect to return."[18] Others put if differently, but the meaning was equally clear: they were determined to be free and were aware of the existence of territory where they could find that freedom. Interviewed in 1863, William Cornish recalled that he had come to Canada in 1856 from the Eastern Shore of Maryland not because he was abused; "I came here just for freedom," he declared. A fellow Maryland slave, Henry Williamson, echoed Cornish's sentiment when he told Benjamin Drew that he "wanted to be free." Richard Newman has called this "a free soil consciousness," and Sue Peabody a "free soil principle."[19] Lord Dunmore was aware of this when he issued his proclamation in 1775 at the start of the Revolutionary War offering freedom to any slave who would throw in his lot with the British. In issuing the proclamation, Dunmore opened up free territory to which slaves flocked in numbers that startled both their former owners as well as those who were leading the fight against the British. The speed and size of the exodus from plantations were best captured in the imagery used by W. E. B. Du Bois in his discussion of those who abandoned plantations and their masters in the early years of the Civil War: it was, he wrote, "like thrusting a walking stick into an ant hill."[20]

Throughout the Americas, the existence of free land or the promise of freedom prompted slaves to abandon their owners. As Jane Landers has shown in her discussion of running away in the eighteenth century, long before the existence of the UGRR, "hundreds of Africans risked their lives to flee southward—to Spanish Florida," responding to the offer and promise of freedom. One Texas slaveholder who, like his contemporaries had lost hundreds of slaves to the free soil of Mexico, may have spoken for many slaves when he lamented, the "negro he has got Mexico in his head."[21]

The knowledge and awareness of free land and the desire for

freedom dominate the testimony and the actions of former slaves. John Henry Hill called on those he left behind in Virginia to follow this historical calling: "Come Poor distress men women and come to Canada where colored men are free." John Clayton echoed these sentiments. A worker in a Richmond tobacco factory, Clayton, thirty-five, escaped with James Mercer and William H. Gilliam in February 1854 by hiding in a small space next to the boiler of a steamer bound for Philadelphia. Soon after, he wrote Still: "You may rest assured that I feels myself a free man and do not feel as I did when I was in Virginia thanks be to God I have no master into Canada but I am my own man."

Seventeen-year-old Rebecca Hall left Baltimore in August 1855 because, as she told Still, "she wanted to be free." Robert Jones, thirty-five, and his wife Eliza, forty, left Petersburg Virginia, in the same month as Hall. Jones reported that he left because he "wanted his liberty—always had from a boy." Not long after he arrived in Canada, Jones organized the Queen Victoria Rifle Guards, a black military company, in which he, John Henry Hill, and Hezekiah Hill served as officers. Away from the system, those who were once slaves came together to express their sense of freedom in ways unimaginable just a few short years earlier. These were expressions of political, economic, and psychological independence, the ability to frame one's life and future untrammeled by the dictates of a master.[22]

To even the most casually observant slaveholder in the mid-nineteenth century the slave system seemed to be hemmed in by a wall of free territory about which their slaves were aware. To the north lay the Free States and Canada, to the southeast and south the recently emancipated territories of the British Empire, and to the southwest Mexico. Efforts by the American government to win concessions from the British through treaties failed to stem the tide of escapes into Canada. Whatever Texas slaveholders tried proved to be equally futile, as were efforts in contested territory such as Kansas, where some Indian peoples were not inclined to respond positively to the entreaties and blustering of Missouri slaveholders. Finally, there were the islands of the British West Indies, particularly the Bahamas and Jamaica, that lay close to major U.S. shipping lanes. Slaves consciously exploited these points of vulnerability to effect their escapes. Although it is next to impossible to quantify the number of slaves who decided to head south rather than north, the evidence suggests that escapes along the Atlantic seaboard to islands such as Jamaica were not infrequent.

One incident that took place in 1855 shows both the inventiveness of the slaves and those who helped them when planning escapes and the impact their actions could have on relations between Washington and London. Relations between the two capitals had long been strained over the refusal of British authorities to return slaves on ships that had been driven by bad weather to take refuge in the Bahamas or Bermuda. In 1831 the brig *Comet* ran aground on a Bahamian island with 164 slaves on board. Three years later another brig, the *Encomium*, with 45 slaves, ran into similar difficulties. The following year the *Enterprise*, with 78, slaves was forced into Hamilton, Bermuda, by bad weather. In all three cases American authorities called unsuccessfully for the release and return of the cargoes, including the slaves. In another case, that of the *Creole*, it was a revolt by slaves and not bad weather that forced the ship into Nassau, Bahamas. Although Bahamian authorities were willing to hold for trial those who were involved in the revolt, in none of these cases, whether it was the action of slaves or the result of inclement weather that forced the ships into port, were the slaves returned.[23]

In May 1855 a crowd in excess of 300 gathered on the wharf of Savanna-la-Mar, Jamaica, when it was rumored that there was a slave on board the brig *Young America*, which had recently arrived from Baltimore. Word spread rapidly that Samuel Rogers, the ship's captain, had confined the slave on board, worried that an attempt would be made to rescue him. Rogers had grounds to be concerned. Although the gates to the wharves were closed to prevent access to the ship, a crowd of men and women got around this barrier by launching a number of rowboats from a beach nearby. Within minutes the slave was taken on board one of the boats, which brought him to shore, where he was taken into custody. The next day the slave was set free following a brief appearance before Justice R. F. Thomas in the Court of Petty Sessions.

Behind this simple outline lies a complex story. Prior to leaving Baltimore, Captain Rogers had hired on as a cook Phillip Nettles, reputedly a free black from the city, paying him $23 in advance. Before the ship could clear the Chesapeake Bay, however, Rogers realized he had made a terrible mistake: Nettles could not cook, which raised suspicions about his true identity. When confronted, Nettles first stuck to his story. Had he not shown Rogers his free papers and so proved his status as a free man who could be hired without violating any state or local laws? But under constant badgering Nettles was finally forced to admit he was not who he claimed to be. He was John Anderson—he is sometimes referred to as Joseph or James in reports—a twenty-five-year-old Baltimore slave who had been hired out by his owner, a Mr. Robinson, for many years and so had lived relatively freely, as did many others in the port city. His friend Nettles, a free black, had lent him his free papers. Complicating the picture even further is the fact that Anderson had been brought on board by his "landlord and a young woman." The implication is that the landlord was white. At a time when local observers worried about the existence of elements of the UGRR in the city, it seems that Anderson had the help of Nettles, his landlord, and the unnamed woman in planning his escape. It was the sort of alliance that haunted southerners. Captain Rogers faced two problems. First, he knew that under Maryland law and Baltimore ordinances, he would be held liable for Anderson's escape even if he could prove he had been duped. Second, he was determined to recover the $23 he had paid Anderson. He concluded that the best way to resolve both problems was to keep Anderson on board rather than put him ashore in Norfolk or at some other port along the coast, where he would be forced to answer potentially embarrassing questions.

Once the ship dropped anchor in Jamaica, the drama took a new if not unexpected turn. As a frequent visitor to Jamaica, Captain Rogers knew he was likely to lose Anderson. In a similar incident two years earlier, two Charleston, South Carolina, slaves, H. A. Handy and William Lewis, were freed from the *Paraguay* when it docked in Kingston. The freeing of Handy and Lewis and the refusal of the local authorities to hand over American fugitive slaves who had escaped to British territories meant that Rogers knew he was unlikely to get his way. His problems were compounded by the fact that he knew he would probably face prosecution in Maryland for allowing Anderson to escape. Keeping Anderson below deck and out of sight, then, seemed the best thing to do in an untenable situation.

Once it became known that Anderson was being held on board the ship, a group of Jamaicans went before a local magistrate and insisted he declare the slave free. But the magistrate refused to act, insisting that it was the sole responsibility of the people to whom the ship was consigned to take the initiative. In light of this ruling, the consignees sent for Captain Rogers, who in an attempt to prove Anderson was who he initially claimed to be, provided what were called "protection papers" signed by a notary in Baltimore stating that the man who came on board the *Young America* was Phillip Nettles, a free black. Rogers calculated that if he could show the courts that he honestly believed the person he had hired was Nettles, a free man, and acted on that belief, then there was no reason why a free man should be brought before the magistrate against his will. It was a long shot. And even if the magistrate bought his rather tortuous reasoning, Rogers knew that the decision would be appealed. But Rogers may also have been counting on such a delay to provide him with time and a cover to set sail from Jamaica unmolested.

The rescue and the hearing before the magistrate generated a great deal of public interest locally and raised conflicting questions about the international reach of American laws meant to address domestic issues. Even to some observers who opposed slavery, forcefully freeing Anderson from an American ship, flying an American flag, which was considered American territory, was a "violation of international law." If that were the case, a supporter of the rescue countered, and the "offence" was committed on American soil, would Anderson have to be handed over for trial in the United States? Such a conclusion would be preposterous, he insisted, as it would first have to ignore the fact that, at the time of the rescue, the ship was anchored in British waters. Once in British territory, he argued, everyone on board became answerable to British law "in the same manner as British subjects must conform to American laws in American ports and on American territory, even to be locked up in the 'Calaboose,' if they happen to be dark, till their departure." What was sauce for the goose was sauce for the gander, for under the laws of many southern states, black foreigners in ships docked in their ports were held, sometimes in prison, until the ship departed. But more to the point, he concluded, slavery is a form of kidnapping, and Jamaicans should have nothing to do with such illegal acts. "It matters not where from, in order to render the kidnapper amenable to our laws; and any person held in slavery in our territory, or in our waters, is kidnapped, without any reference to the laws of the country whence he comes."[24]

Such legal niceties mattered little to Robert Monroe Harrison, the U.S. consul in Kingston, for whom the storming of the ship, the rescue of the slave, and the action of the magistrates were direct assaults on American property and a violation of international law. He demanded that the Jamaican governor conduct a full and impartial inquiry. In the meanwhile, Harrison kept his superiors in Washington fully informed of developments, especially Jamaican public opinion. In the years since his appointment as consul in 1832, this proud Virginian had kept up a constant stream of vitriolic criticism of West Indian emancipation, which he insisted had lead to economic decline and social and political chaos in the island. The specter of racial equality and the emergence of black Jamaicans in leadership positions alarmed and galled Harrison. He viewed with dismay what he believed was the emergence of an alliance between blacks, mulattoes, and "a few jews who are such a *cowardly* set of wretches that fear alone makes them stick to the mulattoes." Harrison never missed an opportunity to pour scorn on the alliance. The investigation, he hoped, would deter "not only the savage Negroes from insulting our fellow citizens, but unprincipled magistrates from abetting them in their villainous acts." The most vociferous supporters of the mob action on the wharf, he declared, were the editors of the *Morning Journal,* a "wooly headed Sambo and quadroon." Harrison spent a great deal of time and energy conjuring up the most lurid and insulting epithets of those who condoned the actions at Savanna-la-Mar. They were nothing if not "half savage negroes and magistrates, who as far as I can learn, were for the most part people of colour and natural sons of Jews by Negroes and Mulattos, prejudiced against everything American but negroes and their descendents."[25] Emancipation was an experiment with such dire social and economic consequences, he warned consistently, that the United States should avoid it at all costs.

There was another consequence of West Indian emancipation that seemed to haunt Harrison: he was convinced that, in an effort to destroy slavery in the United States, the British had frequently dispatched abolitionist emissaries from Jamaica to America. Following the rescue of Handy and Lewis, he insisted that they were "induced to fabricate" their claims to freedom by a "petty fogging Lawyer who was in the United states about a year ago lecturing on Slavery in various parts of the country by the name of William W. Anderson." There is no evidence that William Anderson, a Scotsman and lawyer long resident in the island, was doing any such thing; he had been sent to the United States by Jamaican plantation owners to encourage black Americans to migrate to Jamaica.

But the frequent visits of black and white American abolitionists to the island since emancipation, as well as missions like William Anderson's, was proof enough, as far as Harrison was concerned, of the existence of an abolitionist conspiracy aimed at destroying American slavery. Harrison's claims of an international conspiracy against American slavery seemed to be reinforced by regular commentaries and letters to the editor of Jamaican newspapers that placed the rescue of Anderson in the wider context of political developments in the United States, especially community resistance to enforcement of the 1850 Fugitive Slave Law. With an eye on a failed attempt to rescue a slave named Anthony Burns in Boston a few months earlier, "A Freeman" had asked rhetorically, "if you sympathize, and probably would have taken part, with the worthy Bostonians, had you been amongst them, in their fruitless endeavours to rescue the slave from the grasp of the oppressor, how can you find fault with precisely a similar act in a seaport in free Jamaica?" Not only was it the right thing to do in spite of the constant carping of the "sensitive Yankees" about violations of the American flag, he reasoned, the actions of the rescuers were a clear reaffirmation of the island's determination to protect its nationals as well as a message that Jamaicans would no longer tolerate, as they had in the past, American slaveholders coming to Jamaica and acting with impunity.[26]

"A Freeman" also reminded his readers of the occasions on the eve of emancipation when free blacks were taken from Montego Bay by Americans and sold into slavery. There was an even more recent case, which, surprisingly, he did not mention. In May 1853, African Americans and sympathetic whites in Pittsburgh, Pennsylvania, got word from the Pennsylvania Abolition Society in Philadelphia that Thomas J. Adams from Montgomery County, Tennessee, just north of Nashville, was on his way to Pittsburgh by train, along with a black youth named Alexander Hendrickure, who they suspected had been kidnapped. A large crowd met the train when it arrived in Pittsburgh. Adams was taken into custody, and Hendrickure was freed under a writ of habeas corpus. Adams was later freed when he agreed to give up the youth. As it turned out, while on a stopover in Jamaica, Adams had persuaded the young Jamaican to accompany him to the United States with promises of opening riches for him in California. The evidence suggests, however, that his plan was to sell Hendrickure into slavery in Kentucky.[27]

To "A Freeman" such incidents justified the rescue of Anderson as both an act of abolitionist solidarity and a defense of the island's citizens from potential abduction. But the Anderson case also provides an opportunity to widen our lens the better to understand the range and scope of responses to the Fugitive Slave Law. Soon after the law's enactment in September 1850, a meeting held at the Bible Depository in Bridgetown, Barbados, adopted a series of resolutions expressing abhorrence of the "spirit of the act, the principles on which it was passed, and the objects it was intended to accomplish." The meeting also made plans to collect funds to help fugitive slaves in "affecting their escape from such injustice, tyranny and oppression."[28] The meeting may have articulated the sentiments of many in the region. But to some Jamaican observers the Anderson case raised thorny questions about the consequences of resistance to established law. The editors of the *Colonial Standard*, for instance, echoed the views of those in the United States who feared that resistance to any duly enacted law would inevitably result in political anarchy. "A riotous rabble," the editors insisted, "had no more right to board an American vessel in order to rescue a slave, than they would have had to commit the same outrage, in order to take a white seaman articled to the ship from before the mast." Even the editors of the Falmouth *Post*, who thought Anderson should have been freed, wondered about the consequences of popular resistance to laws however heinous they might be. Put in the starkest terms, illegal action could under no circumstances be condoned even if its aim was the laudable freedom of a slave. Anyone, who "outraged the laws" opened themselves to "prosecution and punishment," the editors suggested. A slave had every right to try to escape, but the people of Savanna-la-Mar could not "set up a law of their own, in opposition to the law of the land, for the purpose of 'freeing a brother in captivity.'"[29] The nicety of the argument was lost on supporters of the action, for as "A Freeman" countered, slavery was morally if not legally akin to kidnapping. Much of the hearing in the Court of Petty Sessions was devoted to an examination of whether the "rabble" had acted riotously. Anderson was removed from the ship while Rogers was on shore, and there is no evidence that the five men who took him threatened anyone on board the ship, although one would be surprised if those on board considered themselves a friendly welcoming committee. All of those who witnessed the events on shore admitted that women in the crowd treated Captain Rogers roughly, in one case snatching the "protection papers" from him. But there was a general consensus that the crowd, made up of a "mixed concourse of different classes of people," many of them women, was on the whole peaceful. Harrison had met a similar reception at the end of the hearing for Handy and Lewis when a crowd made up mainly of women "hooted and hissed" at him.[30] This description of the crowd that greeted Anderson makes it sound very much like the groups who attempted to protect fugitive slaves from recapture in the United States. They were large, a mixture of men and women, boisterous, but above all else convinced that the slave should be free.

Although experience told Harrison he had little chance of winning the return of Anderson, he insisted that the governor order an inquiry. Within days, the custos (or mayor) of Westmorland (the parish in which Savanna-la-Mar is located) submitted a report on the incident to Governor Henry Barkley, who agreed with many of its findings. The excitement, as he delicately described the events that took place on the wharf, was caused by Captain Rogers not allowing Anderson to come on shore. It was very likely Rogers would have gotten redress for the attacks by men on his ship and by the women on shore had he applied to the authorities. In the end, Barkley wondered what more could be done beyond calling on magistrates to be more cautious and to act less precipitously in the future. Not surprisingly, Harrison vigorously opposed both Barkley's reasoning and his conclusions, but in the end, he could do no more than hope that, in the future, magistrates would be prevented from acting as they did and that the perpetrators of such riots would be brought to justice. Harrison believed that the governor must have known that such a "national insult" should only be addressed by the respective governments and not by two or three "prejudiced Magistrates of Colour who were themselves implicated in the matter, and were in reality the cause of the insult to our Flag." Falling back on his customary view of what motivated the island people in their relations with the United States, Harrison was not very optimistic that anything would be done to prevent similar events in the future. From his "knowledge of the character of the inhabitants of the West Indian colonies, and more specifically those of this Island, who are more hostile to us than any other class of people I have met," he concluded, almost in despair, that "the abduction of black or coloured persons from our vessels will never cease unless our Government address England on the subject in terms not to be mistaken." But Americans also had to be more vigilant if they ever hoped to defend their property against a combined assault from slaves and their abolitionist instigators. Following the Handy and Lewis incident, Harrison had written collectors at the main ports in the United States, calling on them not to allow black seamen to ship out on vessels, especially those bound for the West Indies and South America. Such was the "power and audacity of the Negro and coloured population here just now," he had warned, "heightened and stimulated by a plentiful distribution of Uncle Tom's Cabin that I feel certain that they would take any of their colour out of an American Vessel be they free or otherwise!" The U.S. government could have followed Harrison's suggestion and taken the dispute before the joint commission set up by the United States and Britain to deal with such cases, but in the end it chose not to do so. Following receipt of Barkley's report, the British Colonial Office concluded cryptically, "It does not seem possible that the US Government can make anything of this case.[31]

The Anderson case is eerily similar to that of another fugitive slave, also named John Anderson, who fled to Canada at the end of the 1850s to avoid prosecution for murder. Arrested and brought before the Court of Queen's Bench, Anderson was finally freed on a technicality following intense public pressure on the British government organized by the British and Foreign Anti-Slavery Society.[32] Both cases also raise intriguing questions about the political reach of American fugitive slave laws and the many ways opponents found to resist their enforcement at home and abroad. Like Banks and many others before them, Anderson, Handy, and Lewis took the decision to act, and their actions were a direct political challenge to slavery. Banks and Anderson knew this, and so did Handy and Lewis. They had a profound sense of the meaning of freedom. When asked by the magistrate in Savanna-la-Mar why he went on board the ship in Baltimore, Anderson replied poignantly: "I have been kept in bondage and hearing that this was a free country I tried to get here." Handy was equally clear: "My object for going on board was for the purpose of achieving my liberty."[33] They spoke for all those slaves such as Henry Banks who knew why they were leaving and where they were going. They were engaging in self-emancipation.

2. The Workings of the 1850 Fugitive Slave Law

In August, as Congress put the finishing touches on the Fugitive Slave Law, which, in the eyes of the South, was the political fulcrum on which the entire 1850 Compromise turned, eight slaves from Clarke County in Virginia's Shenandoah Valley arrived in Harrisburg, Pennsylvania, followed closely by their owners and slave catchers. Three of the eight, Samuel Wilson, George Brocks, and Billy, broke their journey in the city, while the others chose to move on further north. The choice to stay in the city was not unusual. The state capital, with a significant black population—at 10 percent the largest of any city in the state—was at the western end of an arc of contested sites of freedom that stretched from there south through Columbia on the Susquehanna River, then east through Lancaster, and finally to West Chester and Philadelphia in the east. Columbia, primarily because of its location and an "insatiable demand for cheap labor," Carl Oblinger has shown, "attracted fugitive slaves and manumitted blacks fleeing the Border slave states," as did, by extension, other towns along the arc. There were also isolated black communities in rural areas made up mainly of recently freed slaves. The topography of the area, with its mountain ranges running southwest to northeast, was in places remote enough to provide inaccessible sanctuary for those who chose to stay clear of settled areas. It was a region made up of pockets of black rural and urban populations, as well as settlements of Quakers, long a magnet for slaves fleeing Maryland, Virginia, and Delaware. When, for example, James Pembroke, the twenty-year-old slave who would later be known as J. W. C. Pennington, fled from Queen Annes County, Maryland, in 1827, he was directed to the home of the Wrights, a Quaker family in Adams County, Pennsylvania, active in the UGRR. When William and Ellen Craft arrived in Pennsylvania from Georgia in late 1848, they too were directed to a Quaker family on a farm outside Philadelphia and were later aided by the Pennsylvania Anti-Slavery Society to move to Boston.[1]

Wilson, Brocks, and Billy may have felt secure once they reached Harrisburg. One observer estimated that there were close to 150 fugitive slaves living in the city at the time. But their masters were in hot pursuit. On August 17 the three runaways were arrested, charged, and imprisoned for stealing a number of horses, not for being fugitive slaves—a move intended to ease their rendition by not riling the black community. But no one was fooled. Wilson and Brocks were two of William Taylor's twenty-four slaves; Billy was claimed by John E. Page, a fifty-four-year-old farmer and lawyer and the owner of twenty-seven slaves. Six days after their arrest, they were brought before Judge John L. Pearson on a writ of habeas corpus taken out by unnamed members of the black community. They were represented by two of the city's most prominent lawyers and abolitionists, Charles Rawn and Mordecai McKinney. Rawn, a Free-Soil Democrat, was a leading figure in the defense of fugitive slaves. McKinney was a founding member of the Harrisburg Anti-Slavery Society, the first society of its kind in the state, as well as a member of the Pennsylvania Anti-Slavery Society. Rawn and McKinney were hired by William M. Jones—a fifty-nine-year-old black "doctor" and teamster who had owned property in the city since the 1830s, including a large boardinghouse that was known locally as a "temporary haven for fugitives"—and Edward Thompson, a thirty-four-year-old black laborer.[2] Very likely it was Jones and Thompson who procured the writ of habeas corpus for the three fugitive slaves. In the hearing before Judge Pearson, witnesses for the owners were their own worst enemies. George H. Isler, Taylor's neighbor, testified that Wilson, Brocks, and Billy had stolen four horses, which they released to return home a few days later. This, as far as Isler was concerned, was grounds enough to return the three to Virginia as fugitives from justice. Taylor, for his part, admitted that he had offered a reward of $500 for the return of Wilson and Brocks as fugitives from labor. Four black witnesses, including Jones, appeared for the defense, insisting the three runaways had been in town since June, before they were reputed to have escaped with the stolen horses. Two local white witnesses, however, recalled seeing a group of unidentified blacks, as many as eight, crossing a bridge into the city in July. Judge Pearson dismissed the case against the three on the grounds that they had not stolen the horses for profit but only used them to effect their escape, which he considered a form of trespass and not grounds to return them to Virginia as fugitives from justice. But he did allow that, while he had no jurisdiction in fugitive slave cases, the slaveholders had a right in principle to reclaim their property as long as it was done peacefully.[3]

Just before Pearson's summation, a large crowd of African Americans gathered outside the courthouse, determined to prevent Taylor from seizing the fugitives. The details of what followed are not entirely clear. When Taylor and others tried to seize Wilson, Brocks, and Billy as they left the jail, the three resisted. A number of blacks in the crowd tried to intervene, including Joseph Popel, who was beaten bloody by Taylor's group. Wilson and Brocks were also hurt in the melee, but during the scuffle Billy was hustled away by about twenty blacks who later provided him with a pistol and got him out of town. On orders of the court, a sheriff's posse arrested Wilson, Brocks, Taylor, and a number of Taylor's supporters. Arrest warrants were also issued for ten blacks, including Popel, Jones, and Jones's son David, who were charged with rioting, disturbing the peace, attempting a violent rescue of fugitives, and the violent seizure of Billy. Of the ten charged, seven were heads of household. Some, like Jones, were men of property. Twenty-eight-year-old Henry Bradley, for example, was, according to Mary Houts, a "prosperous" barber. Taylor and 10 others were also charged with violating an 1847 Pennsylvania law that aimed to prevent the kidnapping of blacks and attempts to return fugitive slaves by force of arms. Taylor in turn brought charges of assault against the fugitives in an effort to prevent their immediate release.[4]

But before any of the accused could be brought to trial, the Fugitive Slave Act, signed into law by President Millard Fillmore on September 18, changed the political climate surrounding the case. Twelve days after the law was signed, Richard McAllister was appointed by Supreme Court Justice Robert Grier as a commissioner with the power to adjudicate all cases involving fugitive slaves in Harrisburg. McAllister, a Democrat from a prominent local family reputed to be the last to own slaves in Harrisburg, had studied law in Savannah, Georgia. His views on the presence of blacks in Pennsylvania were best summed up in comments he made in a case in which he acted as defense counsel for John Sanders and Solomon Snyder, whom he had earlier appointed as constables and who were accused of kidnapping: "We do not want to make Pennsylvania a place of refuge for absconding slaves or free negroes," he declared, for "they are a miserable population—a tax and a pest."[5] It became clear from the first case to come before him that, as commissioner, McAllister was passionately committed to enforcement of the law. He rarely gave adequate notice of hearings to attorneys such as Rawn. Not once did he entertain, much less accept, opposing views of defense counsels. Slaveholders knew they had a sympathetic commissioner in Harrisburg and beat a regular path to his door in search of their slaves. Under the terms of the law, hearings before commissioners were to be summary, and McAllister, unlike commissioners in other parts of the Free States, ensured that they were. He dismissed all attempts to challenge the terms of a warrant or even the identity of a suspected fugitive slave. In the first few weeks after he assumed office McAllister named a number of constables who were responsible for enforcing his rulings. He was the sort of commissioner on whom slaveholders depended and on whom the success of the law rested.

On the day of McAllister's appointment, September 30, Taylor appeared before the new commissioner with Samuel Wilson and George Brocks manacled. He swore the two were his slaves, and that was good enough for McAllister, who ordered their return. Rawn dismissed the hearing as a farce. There is no report that even the most summary evidence was taken or that Taylor had to provide irrefutable proof that the slaves he claimed were his. Aware of what had happened at the end of the hearing before Judge Pearson, McAllister named Solomon Snyder and Michael Shaeffer to head a posse to return the slaves to Virginia. They in turn hired Samuel Kintzer, Thomas Hubbard, Henry Loyer, and seventeen others to join them, a substantial force meant to overwhelm and intimidate any possible opposition from the black community. Under section 9 of the new law the expenses associated with the work of posses was to be covered by the federal government. The six-day, 191-mile round trip to Clarke County cost the government $263.91.[6] Over the next few months this would become standard practice. At the end of hearings in Harrisburg, slaveholders would ask for the formation of a posse, declaring their concern that the black community would intervene to prevent the return of slaves, and McAllister would comply with their request.

The return of Wilson and Brocks did not end court proceedings associated with the case. Taylor and the others were due to appear in November. According to Rawn, a jury was never empanelled yet the defendants were found innocent. The trial against the ten African Americans was postponed by Judge Pearson until January 1851. Petitions from the city's leading citizens calling for dismissal or leniency may have persuaded Pearson to dismiss the case.[7] About the same time that the case against the ten was dismissed, local newspapers reported that Billy had been arrested near Danville, Pennsylvania, well north of Harrisburg and brought before McAllister. As it turned out, the person who appeared before McAllister was not Billy but David, another of the party who had arrived in Harrisburg with Wilson, Brocks, and Billy but chosen not to remain in the city. The hearing produced one of the more unusual accounts of group escapes. David insisted that he did not know he was running away when he left. He had gone along because he had been invited to a wedding "up the country." He soon learned that talk of a wedding was just a way to get him to join the escaping group. Rather than return, he decided to continue with the group to Pennsylvania. He told McAllister he would have returned long ago had he known the way home. McAllister was eager to oblige and returned David to his owner, Thomas Briggs of Berryville, Clarke County, under escort, at the expense of the federal government, even though there was no evident threat of resistance from the black community.[8]

Seven other cases followed in Harrisburg in quick succession during 1851, a period of rising tension in the North over enforcement of the law. In each case McAllister ruled in favor of the slave masters. The first involved the Franklin family, who had escaped in 1849. Daniel, the slave of Dr. Robert Franklin of Anne Arundel County, Maryland, and his wife Abby and child Caroline, slaves of Barbara Wailes of Baltimore, were captured in Columbia by Snyder and Shaeffer, two of McAllister's constables, in April 1851 and taken to Harrisburg. Since their arrival in Columbia there had been a new addition to the Franklin family. As a result, the case raised the thorny question of separating a ten-month old freeborn child from his parents. McAllister set the hearing for 6:45 A.M. partly, one suspects, to preempt opposition from the black community, which had gotten word that the family had been brought to town. Charles Rawn and Mordecai McKinney asked to have the hearing delayed by one hour. McAllister refused and promptly ruled in favor of the slaveholders on the evidence given by Dr. Franklin's eighteen-year-old son. If the presence of a "suckling child" or the fact that the child was freeborn troubled McAllister, it did not deter him. The law had to be enforced, and if that required the separation of the child from its parents, then so be it. Although friends of the Franklins agreed to keep the child, in the eyes of many McAllister had done what so many slaveholders did: separated a family.[9]

In early August 1851 Elizabeth O'Neill of Havre de Grace, Maryland, requested a warrant from McAllister for the arrest of her slave William Smith, also known as Bob Sterling. Smith had escaped in the spring of 1845, and O'Neill suspected he was living in Columbia. Three days later, Henry Loyer arrested Smith, who was working on a coal boat, and brought him to Harrisburg. Word of Smith's arrival spread, and a crowd of blacks gathered outside McAllister's office before the hearing began. Testimony for the claimant was provided by Matilda Wood, who stated that she had known Smith since he was a boy. A similar statement was made in a letter from Wesley Levy of Havre de Grace. No opportunity was provided for Smith or anyone else to rebut these claims, and he was remanded into O'Neill's custody. Worried that an attempt would be made to free Smith, O'Neill requested protection by McAllister's police. But because of the state's 1847 law that prohibited the use of its jails to hold fugitive slaves, O'Neill was forced to spend the night with Smith at a local hotel. A crowd of blacks milled about outside, and during the night someone set the hotel on fire. The fire was detected and extinguished before it could cause more than minor damage. The next day Smith, accompanied by Loyer, Sanders, and Charles Strine, was put on board a train for Baltimore, where he was handed over to O'Neill.[10]

The following month, John Stoucher, John Bell, Edward Michael, and Fenton Mercer were arrested in Fisherville, Dauphin County, Pennsylvania, on suspicion of participating in the bloody events at Christiana, in nearby Lancaster County, a few days earlier when one Maryland slaveholder was killed and another injured attempting to retake three slaves. The killing and the escape of those suspected of being responsible threw the state and, to a more limited extent, the country into political turmoil. Bell was owned by John L. T. Jones a twenty-eight-year-old farmer of Montgomery County, Maryland; Stoucher by Mary E. Shreve; Mercer by Esther Trundle, who was described in court proceedings as "a lunatic"; and Michael by Hezekiah W. Trundle, a forty-one-year-old farmer and the owner of fourteen slaves. It was clear to Judge Pearson, before whom the four appeared, that the charges were false and a mere pretext to get them to Harrisburg. As a result, the charges were dismissed on the grounds that the warrant was issued without a shred of evidence. While Pearson was in the process of writing out his verdict, three of McAllister's police arrested the four slaves in Pearson's court. Pearson's threat to have the policemen arrested was ignored, and the fugitives were taken to the commissioner's office for a hearing. One local newspaper called McAllister's actions a "palpable outrage" and an insult to the court, but Pearson never followed up on his threat.[11]

Rawn and McKinney attempted to act as counsel for the fugitives, but, as he had done in the past, McAllister simply ignored them or, when he deigned to recognize their presence, insulted them. Instead, McAllister questioned the four directly: were you in your master's service? did you escape from his service? do you want to go back to him?, he asked. When Rawn or McKinney protested that such questions were illegal, McAllister insisted he was acting as "an officer of the United States" as a magistrate would in a criminal case. It was in his power, he declared, to take such an approach, for this was an "ex parte and preliminary proceeding." In other words, McAllister was treating the case as if the men were fugitives from justice. Then he made the legally preposterous claim that "the colored men could have a trial in Maryland." McAllister knew yet chose to ignore the fact that, unlike in a case involving a fugitive from justice in which the accused is handed over to the state for trial, in the case of fugitive slaves they were handed over to their putative owners, who had the power to do with them as they pleased. In the presence of his master, Bell was asked by McAllister if he was Jones's slave and if he wished to return. When Rawn and McKinney protested that Bell's response could not be considered evidence, the commissioner paid them no heed. Both lawyers raised further questions about the nature of the evidence. They challenged the grounds on which Mercer was enslaved, for example, pointing out that Esther Trundle had been a "lunatic for 20 years and there was no evidence that her late husband had left a will when he died 25 years earlier." McAllister dismissed their arguments as irrelevant. He also ridiculed them. McKinney's action, he declared, was "enough to make a dog sick." And when McAllister asked one of the fugitives in front of his owner if he wanted the aid of the attorney and the fugitive declined, the commissioner turned to McKinney: "Why, McKinney, you ain't popular with the niggers." Not surprisingly, the fugitives were remanded to their owners. The entire proceedings were dismissed by one local newspaper as a "ridiculous mockery."[12] Worried about possible interference from the black community, McAllister selected a posse of five, which was headed by Henry Lyne, the borough high constable, and included Snyder, Loyer, Sanders, and Shaeffer, to accompany the escapees and owners to Baltimore. Five more men were added to the group as a precaution and an additional four just to help them get across the river and safely to the train. The cost to the federal treasury was $233.73.[13]

"YZ," an observer of the proceedings, publicly accused McAllister of collusion with the owners. A day after the commissioner's verdict, the Harrisburg Telegraph received a letter ostensibly from the owners praising McAllister and the five-man posse for the safe return of the slaves. They claimed to have found out about the slaves from newspaper accounts. But as "YZ" pointed out, the letter could not have been written by the owners and arrived in time to be published by the newspaper so soon after the case's conclusion. How could the owners have heard of the slaves' arrest from newspaper accounts in time to be present in Pearson's court?, he asked. "YZ" pointed the finger at McAllister, accusing him of being the author of the letter. It seems a poster offering a reward of $800 had been circulating in Harrisburg prior to the start of the case. McAllister's constables had recognized the fugitives from the poster's description but, having no legal way to arrest them as fugitive slaves, contrived the claim of their participation in the Christiana shoot-out as a way to hold them. This gave McAllister time to notify the owners. McAllister then supported a delay in the habeas corpus hearings before Pearson and telegraphed the owners to come to Harrisburg immediately. "YZ" also claimed that the commissioner had accompanied the posse to Baltimore, where the slaves were sold for $3,400 and where he pocketed the $800 reward.[14]

Questions were raised from the very beginning about the way the slaves were captured and the grounds on which they were brought to trial. McAllister's treatment of the lawyers and his refusal to entertain any of their challenges went beyond the need to expedite the case. But he never addressed the accusations, allowing the charge that he had benefited directly from the return and sale of the slaves to slave traders to simmer. He offered an explanation of sorts, however, in a letter to the Treasury Department four days after "YZ" raised the issue of possible collusion. "More fugitives have been remanded by me than any other U.S.Com.," he boasted, and "from the precautions taken" there has been no subversion of the law. "It is much better for the peace and interest of the country," he concluded by way of an explanation, "that proper force should be employed than by a niggardly parsimony that Fugitives should escape and their claimants and the U.S. officers killed."[15]

But McAllister was not only offering an explanation to his superiors and those who mattered politically; he and his constables were also deeply frustrated by the tardiness of the federal government in compensating them for the expenses they incurred when returning fugitive slaves. Section 9 of the Fugitive Slave Law may have articulated the federal government's commitment to the enforcement of the law, but it did not establish a mechanism for compensating those involved in policing the system. How was repayment to be calculated? Who was to determine per diem expenses? Would there be support to cover the cost of boarding and lodging for the posses and the fugitives? These were just some of the questions that went largely unanswered during the first eighteen months after the adoption of the law. The problems over compensation arose soon after the return of Taylor's slaves. The federal authorities were unsure about what was a legitimate expense and even if all expenses should be covered. No one in the auditor's office seemed to have a clue. They sent out letters of inquiry to the district attorney of the Eastern District of Pennsylvania and even to a prominent lawyer in Pittsburgh in an effort to gauge local practices when returning fugitives from justice. Initially, Washington even suggested that, because local authorities were responsible for covering the cost of returning fugitives from justice, they should bear the expenses of returning slaves. But this would have been in direct contravention of section 9. Even after the auditors had acknowledged the federal government's responsibility they frequently questioned the expenses submitted by McAllister and other commissioners. Annotations in the margins of expense returns raised questions about the need for such large posses as those McAllister had appointed, the distance they traveled, the time it took to make the round trip, and the cost per mile they charged. Reactions to expenses submitted for the return of John Stoucher, John Bell, Edward Michael, and Fenton Mercer in October 1851 is a case in point. As we have seen, McAllister had hired a posse that totaled seventeen men, first to get the fugitives to his office safely, then to ensure that they were not rescued, and finally to get them safely across the river to the train station and back to Maryland. Because he could not use state prisons to hold the fugitives McAllister had to find alternative accommodation at what he considered, given the situation, an exorbitant but acceptable price. "The prison charge may seem large," he responded to questions from his superiors, "but *when you consider the odium attached to the business and the danger incurred* from the torch of the incendiary it must appear otherwise." But McAllister's explanation did little to expedite reimbursements for expenses incurred by members of his posses. Before the problems were finally ironed out and rules promulgated sometime in 1852, Elisha Whittlesey, first comptroller of the Treasury, played it by ear. "As no rules and regulations have been promulgated," he responded to one of Snyder's submitted expenses, "I think this account should be paid, in as much as the Judge [John Kane] has given a very full certificate."[16]

While the issue of compensation went largely unresolved, McAllister continued to hear cases against alleged fugitive slaves. In three additional cases in November and December of 1851 the commissioner issued return orders. But McAllister's remit extended beyond Harrisburg, especially into Columbia and Lancaster. He became, in effect, the commissioner of the area. It is not clear if this was because the authorities could not find someone willing to assume the position in those neighboring cities or if McAllister's initial mandate included them. Slaveholders who knew or suspected their slaves were in either Columbia or Lancaster would visit McAllister in search of a warrant. In May 1852 Solomon Snyder, Henry Lyne, and a Mr. Cochran, who is unidentified, were at the center of an incident in Columbia that rocked the area. They had gone to Columbia with Archibald G. Ridgely, who is described in some reports as a Baltimore police officer and in others as a member of the independent police firm of Zell and Ridgely of Baltimore. To many, an independent police force was synonymous with a slave catching firm. Ridgely had obtained a warrant from McAllister for the arrest of William Smith, also known as George Stansbury, and another unnamed fugitive slave who was also in Columbia. Ridgely and the others found Smith stacking lumber in a yard owned by a black proprietor, John Williams, and arrested him. By then, Smith had been living with his family in Columbia for about eighteen months.

What happened next is unclear. Reports partial to Ridgely and the others say they feared for their lives from the dozen or so black workers in the yard, all of whom were armed with axes and appeared threatening. They surrounded the officers, at which point Ridgely took out his gun in an effort to keep them at bay. At the same time Smith was forcefully resisting arrest and in the process got Ridgely's thumb in his mouth and was about to bite it off. In the scuffle that followed and in an attempt to extricate his thumb, Ridgely's gun went off accidentally and Smith was killed instantly. A coroner's report, however, painted a different picture of what occurred in the lumberyard. No attempt had been made by his fellow workers to rescue Smith. But Smith did resist, broke free from Ridgely, and was attempting to flee when he was shot. Those who testified at the coroner's inquest were convinced that Ridgely had shot Smith deliberately in an attempt to stop him from escaping. Ridgely insisted that he offered to give himself up to local police but was advised to leave town because of growing anger among those who had witnessed the shooting. He left the area immediately, taking back roads around York and Strasburg before catching a train to Baltimore.[17]

Ever since the Fugitive Slave Act was signed into law by President Fillmore opponents had predicted such an outcome. It could not be avoided, they insisted, if armed slave catchers were permitted to go into black communities where fugitive slaves had been living, some for many years, where they had started families, where they had been gainfully employed, and where they had established themselves as members of the community. There were close calls in other parts of the North. When in October 1850 two slave catchers from Georgia turned up in Boston in search of William and Ellen Craft, for instance, the black community made clear their willingness to defend the pair at all costs. Dynamite was placed around the home where William was being hidden, and blacks armed themselves in anticipation of an assault on the house. Tensions were defused only when the slave catchers, threatened with their lives, were persuaded to leave town empty-handed. Almost a year later, a handful of former slaves made a bloody stand at Christiana, Pennsylvania, determined to maintain their freedom. Smith's resistance was of a different order, but the result was another incident in which someone lost his life during an attempt to enforce the law. With the events at Christiana still fresh in everyone's mind, the governor of Maryland moved swiftly to defuse tensions by appointing two Marylanders, James M. Buchanan and Otto Scott, as commissioners to investigate the shooting of Smith. Snyder and McAllister testified before the commission. Snyder admitted that Ridgely never showed Smith the warrant for his arrest because Smith, who throughout the inquiry was described as "very strong," did not give him the chance. McAllister insisted that the search for Smith had followed all the required procedures: Ridgely had a valid power of attorney, he had provided ample proof that Smith had escaped, and on the basis of these circumstances the commissioner had issued a warrant for his arrest. Snyder admitted he was holding one of Smith's arms when he was shot. The implication was that Ridgely would not have endangered his partner's life by recklessly shooting Smith at such close quarters. Finally, it was reported that Ridgely had been offered $400 to return Smith alive, a sum he would have forfeited only if his life was in danger. The commissioners concluded that Smith's death was accidental.[18]

Initially, District Attorney John L. Thompson had recommended that Governor William Bigler request the extradition of Ridgely to Pennsylvania, but following the inquiry the two agreed that the requisition be postponed until the conclusion of a local grand jury hearing. But if the Pennsylvania authorities were satisfied with the commission's findings, and hoped that the delay in requesting the extradition would ease political tensions, others were not. Ohio congressman Joshua Giddings called for the erection of a monument in honor of Smith, for the nation, he insisted, had always honored those who died in the fight for freedom. Let a "suitable mausoleum," he wrote, be built for Smith, who "was slain . . . while defending his inalienable right to freedom against a gang of piratical men stealers who dared pollute the soil of Pennsylvania," protected by the "inhuman and infamous" Fugitive Slave Law. He also called for a brief history of Smith's life and the events of his death to be inscribed on the monument so that "the execrations of posterity may rest upon the memory of those who have perverted the powers of government to the base purpose of oppressing, degrading and brutalizing our fellow men." Nothing came of Giddings's suggestion, but the memory of the events that occurred in the Columbia lumberyard lingered and, as we shall see, would have a direct bearing on the political future of some of those who participated in the attempted arrest of Smith.[19]

A few days later, Harrisburg was thrown into turmoil over another slave case. It involved a thirty-two-year-old black teamster, James Phillips, who was arrested at work. A married man with two children, Phillips was accused of having escaped slavery in 1838 as a teenager. Since then he had established a life for himself in the city. Two Virginians testified that they knew Phillips when he was a slave and, although they had not seen him in fourteen years, could still recognize him because of his strong resemblance to "a certain slave family." One of the witnesses for the owner, Augustine G. Hudson, offered some of the most convoluted (if not the most bizarre) reasoning presented at any fugitive slave hearing. Hudson claimed that Phillips was the slave of his father, Dennis Hudson, of Culpeper County, Virginia, who gave the slave "with no bill of sale" to his brother, who in turn sold him to Henry T. Fant of Fauquier County, who then hired Phillips to a Mr. Blackford of Page County. Such breathless testimony, it would seem, should have required a modicum of proof, but McAllister demanded none. As ever, he was anxious to expedite the hearing. Neither McKinney nor Rawn, hired to defend Phillips, was notified of the start of the hearing. McKinney turned up after the hearing was well under way; Rawn arrived even later. When they did appear, McAllister refused to recognize them; and when McKinney demanded to see the documents on which the claims were made, the commissioner refuse and flew into a rage: "I decline having anything to do with you. I am not to be interrupted by every lawyer in town." The commissioner also ordered witnesses not to answer questions about how they had discovered that Phillips was in Harrisburg. When Rawn pointed out that the description of Phillips had been altered on the power of attorney, McAllister responded that it was of no consequence. In an attempt to bring an end to the proceedings, McAllister produced an already filled-out order for Phillips's rendition from his desk. When Rawn observed that this was most unusual, the commissioner replied that "if he waited until the hearing of the case, he would have to stay up all night to make them out." While not surprising for those who were familiar with McAllister's record, the verdict nonetheless came as a surprise to many. Phillips's wife Mary, who attended the hearing along with the couple's children, lost her composure when the verdict was read and her husband was led out in chains.[20]

McAllister handed Phillips over to his owners, who placed him in the city jail for safe keeping, again worried that a rescue might be attempted. The case, as one report observed, had caused a "most intense excitement." The streets were "filled with citizens of both sexes." But there was little chance those gathered in the streets could free Phillips. Whereas, in the past, fugitives awaiting return had to be housed in hotels and other places at the expense of the owners, now, because of the recent repeal of the 1847 state law, they could be held securely in the city's jail. The next day, Phillips was put on board a train for Richmond, where he was sold to a slave trader for $505. While he waited to be shipped further south, Phillips penned a letter to his wife from the Richmond slave pen, pleading with her to get his Harrisburg employer, a Mr. Brant, to raise the $900 his new master, William A. Branton of Richmond, was asking. Brant contributed $300 to a fund that a "group of Harrisburg whites" had started soon after McAllister's decision. Once the group succeeded in raising the asking price, Rawn was sent to Richmond to retrieve Phillips and return him to his family and friends.[21]

Gerald Eggert has argued that the remanding of slaves from Harrisburg came to an abrupt halt following the Phillips case. McAllister and those associated with him lost all credibility as a result of the eagerness with which the law was enforced. His decision to return Phillips may have been the straw that broke the camel's back. Not only was the evidence presented at the hearing suspect, but Phillips had been for fourteen years a hard-working resident of the city, where he was well known, had raised a family, and had been a productive member of the black community. The speed with which the money was raised to ransom him is testimony to his standing in the city. And surely his case made some people wonder why there was no statute of limitations on the return of fugitives. The problem may have been larger than McAllister, but by his position and his actions he had placed himself squarely at the center of the dispute. At the heart of the opposition to the Fugitive Slave Law was the black community, which, ever since the case involving the Taylor slaves, had made its presence felt. They were there at hearings in Judge Pearson's court and in McAllister's office, although the commissioner did all he could to limit their presence and make conditions uncomfortable for those who represented suspected fugitives. Hearings were confined to his small office, which measured 6 by 9 feet, in which no desks or tables were provided for defense counsels, who, as one report observed, "were obliged to take notes, if any, as best they could, on their hats, hands or otherwise." Members of the community raised the money to hire Charles Rawn and Mordecai McKinney to defend accused fugitives. They also maintained a presence outside the courts. Following the return of the Taylor slaves, a meeting of African Americans established a committee of five to assist fugitive slaves passing through the city, as well as those who wished to remain. These sorts of organizations were not always permanent. In many cases they were formed to meet a pressing emergency, only to disband when the danger receded. But they could just as easily be mustered again in the face of new dangers. They also could call out a crowd at short notice to bear witness to their continued opposition to the rendition of slaves. During the Franklin family case in April 1851, one local reporter recalled, "the colored portion of the community" were summoned from "the lanes and alleys of the suburbs as suddenly as if they had been but waiting the sound of some tocsin, as a signal for a rush pell-mell towards the residence of Commissioner McAllister." As we have seen, when William Smith (Bob Sterling) was being held at a local hotel before being returned, someone had attempted to set the hotel on fire.[22]

The killing of Smith in Columbia and the speed with which all fugitives who came before McAllister were remanded over the course of less than two years since the adoption of the Fugitive Slave Law made the commissioner and his officers politically unpalatable. Henry Lyne, the high constable, and the three regular constables, Loyer, Snyder, and James Lewis, all Democrats, were elected in local elections in 1852. Although city elections were dominated by Democrats in this period, when the four ran for reelection in 1853, the results were different. All of them, with the exception of Lewis, had been involved in the series of fugitive slave cases. Lyne, Loyer, and Snyder lost; Lewis was reelected with 79 percent of the vote. Lyne stood again in the three subsequent yearly elections and each time lost by large margins. Snyder and Loyer declined to face the electorate again. Of the three, Snyder had developed the most unenviable record. Not only was he involved in slave catching and renditions, he stood trial in 1851 for kidnapping four blacks (though he was acquitted by the jury). He would continue these activities after 1852. Twice in the next few years he was arrested for kidnapping blacks, once in Harrisburg in February 1855 and again in Lancaster four months later. In a report to a New York newspaper, "Keystone" described Snyder as an "inveterate slave hunter [who] has largely escaped the penalty of the law on two or three former occasions."[23]

Although McAllister was appointed to his position and so did not have to face the electorate, he too came under enormous pressure for the way he ran the commissioner's office and the way he seemed to relish returning suspected fugitive slaves. His boast to federal authorities in October 1851 that all those who came before him were remanded after the most cursory hearings did not help him at home. When it was rumored he was contemplating resigning in June 1852, one local newspaper that had grown increasingly skeptical of the law's efficacy and McAllister's role in its enforcement was convinced that, should he resign, "no decent man in Harrisburg will accept the place." The editors of the Telegraph had taken the pulse of the city and could testify to McAllister's growing unpopularity. When he ran in the election for delegates to the State Democratic Convention in August 1852, McAllister failed to carry a single ward in the city. He had also lost favor with members of the Episcopal church in which he served as a vestryman. Both he and the church came under pressure because of his work as a commissioner. Evidently, he was reelected to the vestry by only one vote in 1852 and was told he would have to resign his position as commissioner if he hoped to remain on the vestry. McAllister resigned as commissioner in March 1853. With the election of Franklin Pierce, a fellow Democrat, to the presidency the following year, McAllister hoped his record as a commissioner would result in a federal appointment. One Georgia newspaper supported his claim because he had "stood by the South" and had done more than any other northern man to enforce the Fugitive Slave Law. McAllister supposedly visited Washington, D.C., in his bid for an appointment but returned home empty-handed. Some of his staunchest supporters in Pennsylvania were not surprised he had failed in his quest. Although he was a "singular genius," as one Democratic editor described him, his reputation was destroyed by the passion he brought to his job as a commissioner. Far from "giving confidence in the law," the editor concluded, "his excessive zeal has had a tendency to render it odious." Following his resignation as commissioner, McAllister moved to Kansas, where he later became deputy secretary to the governor with responsibility for ending John Brown's guerrilla activities in the territory. Later in the 1850s he moved to Keokuk, Iowa, where he practiced law.[24]

But McAllister's prospects were also wrapped up in broader political developments surrounding the law and its enforcement in the state. The inability to use state prisons to hold fugitives slaves who were awaiting return had led to a concerted effort to rescind the 1847 state law prohibiting such use. In early 1851 efforts to repeal the sections of the law dealing directly with the use of prisons to hold fugitives failed by razor-thin margins. The senate voted in favor of repeal sixteen to fourteen, but a two-thirds vote was needed, by the rules of the senate, to take up the matter. To supporters of the Fugitive Slave Law, the 1847 law, which they described, echoing the language of an earlier dispute, as "the nullification act of 1847," amounted to open obstructionism. The failure to repeal the law also had national consequences. "No state of the Union is more sound on the question of slavery than the Keystone," a Washington, D.C., editor observed, "and we have no doubt it will take the lead in revoking the mad scheme of the abolitionist agitators by repealing their abolition law, passed under a state of unprecedented excitement." There was growing pressure on state lawmakers and especially Governor William Johnson, a Whig, to repeal the law, which many believed was "essential to the execution of the congressional act on the subject of fugitives." The state Whig convention of 1851 expressed its support for the Fugitive Slave Law by a large margin. And a Harrisburg editor partial to President Fillmore and with an eye on what had transpired in the city, condemned the 1847 law because, he wrote, it endangered fugitives and encouraged mob violence. But Johnson would not budge on either law. He opposed the Fugitive Slave Law as unnecessary and dismissed the arguments of those who believed it was the last best chance of keeping the country together. In the midst of that year's election campaign for governor, and before the Christiana shoot-out changed the political landscape, Johnson pocket vetoed an amendment of the 1847 law. Johnson was defeated in that year's gubernatorial election by William Bigler, a Democrat, who in his inaugural address promised to sign the amendment repealing section 6 of the 1847 law and to resist opposition to the Fugitive Slave Law, for, as he argued, together they "engendered hostile feelings between the different sections of the Union."[25]

Over the next few years, a number of proposals were submitted to the Pennsylvania legislature that aimed to ease the concerns of southern slaveholders that the state was hostile to their interests. In 1853 a Democratic senator from Lycoming County proposed that slaveholders be allowed to bring their slaves into the state if they were in transit. Two years later the House judiciary committee, in a split vote, rejected a similar proposal, with the majority arguing that, under the law of nations and the Constitution, slaveholders already possessed that right, and the minority contending that slavery was a local institution and as such was not recognized by "the law of nature, the common law, or the civil law." In addition, competing petitions were regularly presented to the legislature from groups who were opposed to the settlement of African Americans in the state and those who rejected such an exclusionary proposal. A petition from Philadelphia and Bucks County in 1857, for example, justified the call for exclusion because of the "trouble, inconvenience and expense on account of runaway *niggers* from other states." Others called for a complete ban on the settlement of mulattoes and Negroes, free or otherwise, in the state.[26]

Although none of these proposals resulted in laws that denied the right of free African Americans to come into the state, political sentiment generally continued to favor the vigorous enforcement of the Fugitive Slave Law. It is this commitment to the law that lay behind the drive to repeal section 6 of the 1847 law that denied authorities the use of state prisons to hold remanded slaves. But the limited reach of the repeal also reflected deeper concerns about the frequent kidnapping of free blacks from the state, which the 1847 law was also meant to address. In the heated debate leading up to the passage of the Fugitive Slave Law opponents had predicted that, because it denied accused fugitive slaves the right to a trial by jury, it increased the chances that African Americans who were born free but could not immediately prove they were free would fall victim to kidnappers. Although kidnappings from Pennsylvania's southeastern counties were not uncommon before 1850, fears of an increase in their frequency seem to have been borne out by developments in the months after the passage of the law. William Kashatus has counted at least "a dozen kidnappings" in Chester County in the six months after the passage of the law. There was a pattern to these operations. A group of armed white men would attack the home of a black family while they slept, nab one of the occupants, place the person in a carriage, and race to the Maryland line to catch a train for Baltimore, where they hoped to—and many times did—sell the person to a slave trader. In many instances, black neighbors attempted to foil the plan. White neighbors sometimes followed in the hopes of intercepting the group before they got to Baltimore or tried to retrieve the kidnapped blacks from slave pens before they were sold.[27]

There were also organized bands of kidnappers within the state. The most notorious was the Gap Gang, centered in the town of Gap, just north of Christiana, which operated in western Chester and southeastern Lancaster counties. On a lecture visit to Gap in early 1851, C. C. Burleigh, the abolitionist, reported on the depredations of the gang and efforts of African Americans to resist its activities. "The colored people," he reported, "were desperately resolved on self-defense against the land pirates, which have been let loose upon them by the recent Slave catching Law." The gang participated in a wide array of illegal activities beyond kidnapping, including horse stealing, counterfeiting, receiving stolen goods, burglary, incendiarism, and hunting fugitive slaves. Attempts by local and state authorities to break up the gang met with little success. In 1854 many were optimistic that the "dangerous band of villains" was on the verge of being disbanded when a few of its members were arrested and its leader, the "notorious kidnapper" William Bear, was forced to flee to Maryland, "that refuge of kidnappers." In spite of this success, the gang was still in operation two years later, however, when nine of its members were arrested, among them John Townsend, "a man advanced in years" and the owner of a sawmill in Penningtonville. Clearly, one report had to admit, many of the gang's members were still at large.[28]

The most sensational incident in the area involved the kidnapping of two young sisters, Elizabeth and Rachel Parker, from Chester County in late December 1851. Both girls lived in West Nottingham Township in the southwestern corner of the county, a mile or two from the Maryland line. The group of kidnappers was led by Thomas McCreary, thirty, from Elkton, Maryland, fifteen miles from the Pennsylvania state line. For some years he had been the mail carrier between Elkton and Chestnut Level, Pennsylvania, and in addition his brother lived near the Parkers, so he was familiar with the area: he knew the sisters were free, knew the neighborhood where they were raised, and knew the persons in whose home they worked. McCreary also had a history of kidnapping; he was suspected of a kidnapping in Dowingtown in 1848 and two in Unionville the following year. McCreary adopted a simple mode of operation. He would wait outside the home alone or with an accomplice until his victim came out, while another accomplice waited in a carriage close by. One of his known confederates was John Merritt, twenty-one, formerly of Pennsylvania but in 1851 living, like McCreary, in Cecil County, Maryland. McCreary would nab his victims, place them in a carriage, and race across the state line to catch a train for Baltimore, where the victims would be lodged in the slave pen of Walter L. Campbell, owner of one of the leading slave trading firms in the city. Campbell and his brother also owned a pen in New Orleans, to which they shipped slave cargoes from Baltimore, as well as a farm eighty miles from New Orleans where slaves not sold at the pen were "acclimated to the Southern Market."[29]

Elizabeth, about ten years old, was kidnapped by McCreary and an unnamed man from the home of Matthew Donnelly where she was working, taken by wagon to Elkton, Maryland, and from there by train to Baltimore and housed in Campbell's pen. John Merritt was working at Donnelly's at the time and was clearly a party to the kidnapping, as was possibly Donnelly himself. McCreary claimed he was hired by A. L. Schoolfield, a Baltimore lottery dealer, to reclaim his slaves who had escaped four years earlier. Elizabeth spent two weeks in the Baltimore slave pen before she was shipped off to New Orleans, where she was sold to a woman who owned a large flower garden and for whom she sold flowers and candy. Apparently, Elizabeth convinced a city watchman with whom she had a conversation that she was born free and had been kidnapped and sold into slavery. The man took her to a local magistrate, who demanded an explanation of how Elizabeth was acquired. Word of her whereabouts got back to Chester County, where locals raised $1,500 to purchase her freedom and return her to Baltimore. There new attempts were made to get her to admit she was a slave, but days later, three men from Chester County visited Campbell's pen and gained her release.[30]

One week after Elizabeth was shipped off to New Orleans, McCreary and two unnamed accomplices nabbed Rachel, her older sister, from the home of Joseph C. Miller, a forty-year-old farmer. A visitor later reported that the modest two-story house sat in an isolated part of the township three-quarters of a mile from the nearest neighbor. McCreary followed the familiar route to Baltimore and Campbell's pen, claiming that, like her sister, Rachel had escaped from Schoolfield. Unlike her sister, Rachel did not go quietly. On the way to Baltimore she told anyone she met and who would listen that she was free. She told the landlord at the tavern where the party stopped and several persons at the railroad office. When a man she later described as having "large light colored whiskers" visited her at the slave pen to persuade her to admit she was Schoolfield's slave, she refused; when he threatened to cowhide her and throw her in a dungeon, she boldly insisted she was free; and when, in an attempt to get her to admit she was a runaway, she was told that Elizabeth had confessed, Rachel responded that her sister must have been coerced. That no one on the way to Baltimore was willing to intercede speaks to the ease with which kidnappers such as McCreary operated and the dangers freeborn blacks faced. Yet one can only marvel at young Rachel's determination to resist as best she could.[31]

Unlike Matthew Donnelly, who seemed to have colluded with McCreary in the capture of Elizabeth, Joseph Miller and a neighbor immediately followed in an attempt to cut off the kidnappers before they reached the Maryland line. But they were unsuccessful. The following day Miller and a group of seven neighbors—described by one local newspaper as anything but abolitionists—followed McCreary to Baltimore, where they accused him of kidnapping. McCreary and one of his associates were arrested, but after a hearing they were released, with bail set at $300. Miller and his neighbors may not have given much thought to the possible consequences of their actions. But, after all, it had been less than three months since one Maryland slaveholder was killed and another injured by runaway slaves from Maryland at Christiana. Miller and the others were threatened with revenge for the Christiana deaths. Possibly because of these threats, the Pennsylvanians decided to return home soon after. On the way, Miller disappeared from the train. His friends went in search of him and were told he had stepped off the train either to smoke a cigar or to get some fresh air, as the cars were very muggy. On January 2 he was found hanging from a tree. Because there was suspicion of foul play, Miller's body was disinterred from a spot close to where he had been found hanging and taken to Baltimore for a postmortem and coroner's inquest. The inquest ruled that Miller had committed suicide due to depression, possibly brought on by the fact that he knew Rachel to be a slave and had lied about it. Questions were raised immediately about the hasty inquest and its findings, as well as the way Miller's body had been disposed of at the end of the inquest. If he had hung himself, observers in Pennsylvania and elsewhere in the North wanted to know why there were no bruises found on the body, and they asked why the body was allowed to remain unpreserved for the ten days between when it was found and when the inquest was held, time that would have resulted in extensive decomposition. Soon after the inquest, it was reported, "a hole was dug under the tree where he was found, and coffinless and brutally his corpse so dear to others far away, was thrust into it and covered over." Another sympathetic report reinforced some of the details about the way in which the body was disposed of, saying that it was "thrown into an old box, the cover of which was too narrow by three inches, and buried at a depth of two feet." Weeks later another postmortem was performed, this time in West Chester, by Drs. J. W. Hutchinson and E. V. Dickey, who concluded that Miller had first been poisoned with arsenic, then hung. The new finding unleashed a flurry of accusations across the slavery divide. A Richmond, Virginia, newspaper dismissed the findings as "utterly incredible," the conclusion, it said, of "a strong Abolitionist prejudice or the pretended opinion of Abolition rascals." If it was foul play, the editor wanted to know, why would anyone wait for "the operation of arsenic upon his system"? An abolitionist editor countered that although it had been raining heavily at the time of his death, Miller's clothes were dry. The only logical conclusion, he insisted, was that the body was buried after the arsenic had taken effect and after the rain had stopped.[32]

Defense witnesses at Thomas McCreary's trial insisted that Rachel was in fact Elizabeth Crosus, who with her mother June and sister Henrietta, had escaped from Schoolfield or been "taken off by other persons" in April 1847. They could identify Rachel, they explained, because she looked so much like her mother June. The mother was described as "a light chestnut color," while Elizabeth Crosus was a "shade darker" and Henrietta "nearly the same color." The fact that Elizabeth Parker was described as being "as deep a black as one can imagine" did not seem to bother those whose case was built on their ability to identify the alleged fugitives. Contrary to other witnesses, a Mrs. Martin insisted that Rachel was not the girl Elizabeth Crosus who had lived with her at one time. But four or five other witnesses, including Schoolfield's mother and son, pointed to her as the daughter of their slave June, to whom she had a very close resemblance. Both McCreary and Schoolfield's son Luther claimed they heard of Rachel's whereabouts after the capture of her sister Elizabeth. In an effort to undermine the veracity of the testimony of witnesses from Pennsylvania, McCreary's attorneys demanded to know if they had ever been members of societies opposed to the Fugitive Slave Law or of any abolitionist associations. McCreary was acquitted based largely on the testimony of John Merritt, described by some who allegedly knew him as a "worthless and abandoned character" who had been previously tried for counterfeiting and who, according to C. C. Burleigh, had been involved with a gang of depredators—possibly the Gap Gang—who "infested the lower part of Chester County, engaged in gambling, passing counterfeit money, and other swindling operations."[33]

During McCreary's trial, supporters of Rachel Parker petitioned the courts for her freedom in an effort to prevent her being moved or put on a ship for New Orleans. But the petition was also meant to address the difficulty created by the fact that blacks could not testify in Maryland courts when whites were involved, nor could they come into the state to give evidence. As a result, Rachel was forced to petition for her freedom, which in effect put the onus on her to prove she was free rather than getting the court to issue a writ of habeas corpus, which would have shifted the burden of proof onto the claimant. In addition, the Reverend J. M. Dickey and a Reverend Plummer from Pennsylvania visited Schoolfield to plead with him to release Rachel, but they were rebuffed as a "set of abolitionists." Schoolfield would not let her leave prison, where she had been moved from Campbell's slave pen, fearful she would be spirited away and so deny him the chance to prove she was his slave. Rejected, Dickey promised to organize a group of "prominent citizens" to push for her release. Finally, the case came to trial in a Baltimore County court in early January 1853, more than a year after the girls had been kidnapped. Dozens of witnesses from Chester County descended on the Baltimore courthouse at their own expense, among them employers, doctors, and lawyers all of whom claimed they had known Rachel's mother, who had lived near Oxford, Pennsylvania, for almost twenty years, as well as Rachel since she was a baby. The trial lasted eight days, until under the sheer weight of the evidence, Schoolfield relinquished and withdrew his claims to the girls, who were finally able to return home.[34]

In the end, pluck, luck, and organized resistance paid off for the sisters. Rachel's and Elizabeth's refusals to admit they were slaves, McCreary's reputation as a kidnapper, the speed with which the small community in the Nottingham Township rallied to the girls' support, and the attention the cases received in the local and abolitionist media finally led to the sisters' freedom. But coming so soon after the furor over the Christiana crisis, the kidnapping of the girls further increased tension between Pennsylvania and Maryland. It also had the potential of embarrassing Governor Bigler politically. He and the majority of Pennsylvanians had supported the call for an inquiry into what had happened at Christiana, and the federal government had accused those persons suspected of supporting the actions of the fugitive slaves of treason. Why, abolitionists wondered, had the governor or the press not insisted on an inquiry or called on the governor of Maryland to extradite McCreary for the kidnapping of two citizens and the murder of another? In its condemnation of the majority of the state's press, the *Pennsylvania Freeman* put the question boldly: "Do their veins run water?" Even less was heard from the political leaders of the state. The governor did not publicly raise the question of extradition. "There seems to be very little prospect at present," the *Pennsylvania Freeman*'s editor lamented, "that Pennsylvania will utter even a whisper. Shame!" But within two weeks of the editorial the state legislature authorized the governor to hire a lawyer to defend Rachel. Those opposed to the move attempted to buy time by referring the resolution to a committee for investigation. But the attempt to refer the resolution was voted down, the majority insisting that the facts of the case were widely known and incontrovertible. As one senator pointed out, "The state of Maryland, upon the death of Gorsuch [at Christiana], one of her citizens[,]had employed the ablest counsel and dispatched the Attorney General of that State" to litigate the treason trial. Pennsylvania should act similarly. Bigler finally relented under pressure and appointed Thomas S. Bell to work with Pennsylvania Attorney General James Campbell to defend Rachel.[35]

Once the girls were freed in January 1853, the *Pennsylvania Freeman* called on Bigler to set up a grand jury inquest in Chester County to examine the "naked kidnapping." At the same time, friends and neighbors offered a $1,000 reward for the arrest and conviction of Miller's murderer. The pressure on the governor and county authorities seemed to have had the desired effect when, in March, a grand jury in Chester County indicted McCreary and Merritt for murder and Bigler requested the extradition of McCreary (but not Merritt) from Maryland. The exclusion of Merritt from the extradition request struck some observers as unusual if not odd. "Gov [Enoch] Lowe will probably understand Gov Bigler in a Pickwickian sense," the editor of the West Chester *Village Record* declared, "as going through with a mere formality."[36]

In response to Bigler's requisition, Lowe asked for time to consult with the attorneys for Schoolfield and McCreary, as he had been informed there was an agreement between them and the girls' lawyers not to bring a case against their clients, an agreement in effect, Lowe responded, between the state of Pennsylvania and

the defense attorneys. In the end, Lowe refused to extradite Mc-
Creary on the grounds that he had set out to capture Rachel with
the full authority of her master and with the appropriate power of
attorney; he had captured her believing she was a fugitive based
on information received in the area and the "extraordinary like-
ness which exists" between her and Schoolfield's slave, something
commented on by many in Baltimore who also believed they were
one and the same person. Therefore, McCreary was not a criminal
because he had not acted with malicious intent. If he were guilty,
Lowe reasoned, it was "purely technical." Lowe also worried that,
given the prejudice against McCreary in Chester County, he could
not possibly receive a fair trial there. Finally, Lowe enclosed a letter
from James Campbell in which the attorney general had agreed
with lawyers for Maryland that there would be no further prosecution. This, Lowe insisted, was proof of an agreement with the state
of Pennsylvania that the case would go no further.[37]

In a lengthy response, Bigler rejected Lowe's reasoning. If, he
argued, McCreary had followed procedures laid down by the law,
all the problems could have been avoided. Comity demanded
McCreary be handed over, and the fact that the citizens of Chester County were upset because they knew the girls to be free did
not jeopardize McCreary's chances for a fair trial. There was little
doubt McCreary had carried Rachel away in violation of the law.
Bigler was also concerned that Lowe had taken the unusual step of
looking into the record to determine the facts of the case, something that should be a matter for a Pennsylvania jury. Finally, Bigler
rejected the contention that Campbell, in writing to the Maryland
lawyers, was acting for the state. He did not appear at Rachel's trial
in his capacity as the attorney general but as one of the attorneys
named by Bigler. His powers, therefore, were the same as those of
Judge Bell, the other lawyer appointed to defend Rachel. Bigler insisted there was no connection between the trial of the free Parker
girls and the prosecution of McCreary or Merritt.

In spite of his vigorous response, Bigler let the matter drop. He may have decided that Lowe would not budge. But such pragmatism hid a long record of accommodation if not appeasement to slaveholding interests among leading Pennsylvania Democrats, including the governor. At the end of Rachel's trial, Attorney General Campbell had seen fit to issue a gratuitous apology condemning the "foul spirit of abolitionism" and reiterating Pennsylvania's commitment to return fugitives. Bigler himself had come to power riding the wave of revulsion against the Christiana shoot-out, committed to the repeal of the 1847 Pennsylvania law, a law that he had supported when he was in the state senate. Within weeks of his inauguration Bigler had pardoned George Alberti, a notorious Philadelphia slave hunter and kidnapper. Some also wondered why Bigler had not insisted on the extradition of Archibald Ridgely for the killing of William Smith in Columbia or, for that matter, why he had accepted the findings of the Maryland commissioners sent to investigate Smith's death.[38]

The problem of kidnapping and the rendition of fugitive slaves continued to plague relations between Pennsylvania and Maryland throughout the 1850s. Some of the cases involved former officers of the law, men such as Solomon Snyder, John Sanders, and Henry Loyer of Harrisburg who had gained an unenviable record as Richard McAllister's slave hunting constables. All three, along with Jacob Waltman and Daniel Gilland, were indicted by a Lancaster County grand jury in December 1852, charged with kidnapping Fleming Hawkins, a free black. Hawkins claimed he was made drunk and taken in the direction of Maryland but managed to escape his captors. Evidently, Bigler called on Lowe to extradite Sanders, who had fled Pennsylvania once the kidnapping was foiled. There is no report of what became of the extradition request.[39] Snyder and Solomon continued to be involved in efforts to kidnap free blacks. In February 1855, Snyder, with the aid of two African Americans, James Jackson and David Thompson, attempted to kidnap George Clarke, an eighteen-year-old born and raised in Carlisle, Pennsylvania. Jackson and Thompson asked Clarke to help them carry "some things" to a house where there was to be a dance. The house turned out to be Snyder's. When Clarke realized where he was, he tried to flee but was caught. He made enough noise, however, to attract a crowd. Snyder and Jackson were arrested, but Thompson managed to elude capture. Jackson later fled while on bail. Snyder was found guilty and fined $1,000 plus cost and sentenced to six years in prison. He was finally released in May 1858.[40] African Americans, as mentioned, were sometimes involved in the spate of kidnappings that plagued the area. In February 1857, for instance, Jeremiah Logan was hired by Tom Nathans, an African American, to carry goods to the river, where he was seized by a group of men, one of whom was John Sanders. Logan managed to fend them off. Sanders and Nathans were arrested. Some of the other men may have left town, however, after the botched kidnapping attempt. Subsequently, Sanders was indicted, along with George Westfall, Daniel Gilland (who had also been indicted in 1853 by the Lancaster County grand jury), and Thomas Nathans.[41]

S. S. Rutherford has argued that "in the majority of cases where slaves were captured and returned to their master, they owed their betrayal to men of their own color." Rutherford may have exaggerated the extent of black collusion in the recapture of runaway slaves, but there is no doubt in the case of Harrisburg, as Gerald Eggert has shown, that policemen such as Solomon Snyder used paid black spies to "ferret out fugitives in the black community." There is also no doubt that African Americans were sometimes members of kidnapping gangs or sometimes acted independently as kidnappers, occasionally with disastrous consequences. In November 1852, for example, John Anderson, an African American, lured a black boy, John M'Kinney, away from an inn in Maytown on the Susquehanna River, where he was working. A witness reportedly later saw M'Kinney on board a boat leaving Baltimore in early December as part of a group of 150 slaves heading for New Orleans. Anderson was caught and sent to trial, but, unlike the Parker sisters, M'Kinney was lost to a southern plantation.[42]

The depredations of kidnapping gangs in Dauphin and adjacent counties continued throughout the decade. When, in March 1860, John Brown was kidnapped in Chester County and later found in a slave pen in Baltimore, one local newspaper despaired of the history of numerous raids that had taken place in the county and all along Pennsylvania's southern border. Going back to 1820, it recalled the attempt on Jack Reed, who killed his assailant and was later tried for murder but acquitted; the capture from a school in Dowingtown in either 1848 or 1849 (possibly by McCreary) of a girl who was never heard from again; and finally, the five or six African Americans who had disappeared without a trace from the area in the preceding six months. While less frequent, the disappearances from Harrisburg were no less alarming: "There are still men among us," one newspaper reported, "who will steal negroes, and . . . several have been missing of late."[43] Black communities and authorities throughout southeastern Pennsylvania struggled to contain these activities and break up the gangs. The constant threat was just one measure of the vulnerability of black communities in the region. That they fought to protect themselves and sometimes managed to retrieve those who had been kidnapped or those who had been seized in Maryland unaware of the restrictions on free black entry into the state attests to the complex nature of the contest to secure a free space for themselves north of slavery's dividing line.

In spite of these difficulties, the area continued to be a magnet for those seeking freedom from states immediately to the south. Even during the tumultuous early years of the decade there was an unbroken flow of fugitives into southeastern Pennsylvania. They came individually and in large groups. Twenty-six men, women, and children, all owned by Edward Cheney of Funkstown, near Hagerstown, Maryland, entered Lancaster in October 1852, followed by their owner, whom they managed to give the slip. Someone who aided them seemed to take pride in neologisms when he gleefully reported that no trace was found of the "absquated party."

With an eye on recent political developments, another report on the operations of the UGRR in Harrisburg poked fun at the inability of the slaveholders and their minions to locate fugitives. The organization was doing a brisk business in the state capital, it reported: "After their arrival in this place, the fugitives became invisible. They are as hard to find as the 'Know Nothings.' Nobody 'knows nothing' about their whereabouts." The Fugitive Slave Law, the report declared prematurely, was "a dead letter."[44]

Fugitives who entered Harrisburg after 1855 were aided by the Fugitive Aid Society, formed in early 1856 and headed by Joseph Bustill, an African American schoolteacher. One historian has called the society a "neighborhood watch" located in Tanner's Alley, the locus of the black community, where fugitives blended in and lived with free blacks. In its first recorded action, the society sent eight fugitives by rail to William Still, the driving force behind the Vigilance Committee in Philadelphia. The society continued to operate for the rest of the decade. There were regular reports of the movement of runaways through town. Between September and November 1859, for instance, eighteen runaways were aided. Daily they come, one report stated, "several at a time, and the aggregate business of the year is counted by hundreds." If African Americans took the lead and may have acted largely on their own in Harrisburg, in other parts of the state, such as in Chester County, Quakers were also an important component of the organization that assisted fugitives. Kashatus has identified 132 UGRR agents in the county, of which 31 were black, while the rest were Quakers.[45]

Even at the height of the Fugitive Aid Society's successes in the late 1850s it failed to prevent the capture of two suspected fugitives, Daniel Webster, otherwise known as Daniel Dangerfield, in April 1859, and Moses Horner the following March. Both had escaped from Virginia. But because no one was named or could be found to replace Richard McAllister as commissioner in Harrisburg, both cases were initiated and adjudicated in Philadelphia. The owners had to seek warrants from the Philadelphia commissioner, and marshals were sent to Harrisburg to capture the runaways. It made for some interesting connections between the two cities. Black witnesses were brought by train from Harrisburg to testify in support of both of the accused. Webster managed to win his release because the evidence showed clearly that he had been resident in Harrisburg long before he was reputed to have escaped. Horner was not so lucky, in spite of similar claims on his behalf by witnesses.[46]

As if little had changed since the time of the 1850 riot and trials surrounding the Taylor slaves, a few of the principal witnesses in the Webster and Horner cases, such as "Dr." Jones, had been involved in the effort to free Samuel Wilson, George Brocks, and Billy. But both the Webster and Horner cases were, for all intents and purposes, Philadelphia events. What they demonstrate, however, is that even at the height of the success of the Harrisburg Fugitive Aid Society, federal and state officials still had the means to disrupt the life of the black community and those they tried to protect. The level of despair and frustration this must have caused can only be imagined. The message behind Richard McAllister's decisions was unmistakably clear: those seeking freedom from slavery must be and would be hunted down and returned at all costs. The actions of commissioners such as McAllister, buttressed as they were by the federal government, had a decided effect on black communities. The dislocations caused by the Fugitive Slave Law and McAllister's decisions, when coupled with the state government's financial support for the removal of free blacks to the African colony of Liberia, sent a clear message to African Americans that they were not wanted in Pennsylvania. The state legislature's allocation of $2,000 in 1852 to aid the settlement effort in Liberia prompted a month-long debate among Harrisburg's African Americans on the merits of Liberian colonization. Thomas Early, thirty-five, a waiter; John Price, a twenty-eight-year-old shoemaker; and the young student Thomas Morris Chester, whose parents had long been active in the abolitionist movement, which abhorred colonization, spoke in favor of leaving. Samuel Bennett, twenty-seven, a servant; John Wolf, a thirty-two-year-old teacher; and John Pierson, about whom nothing is known, were opposed. Of those in attendance, only Chester actually opted for a future in Liberia.[47] But the mere airing of differences over whether they should leave the country testifies to the levels of frustration and despair that gripped the community in the wake of the 1850 law and its implementation.

If the views of editors are a useful barometer of white attitudes toward the efforts of African Americans to make a future for themselves in the North free from the taint of slavery, then that future was anything but bright. Even editors who opposed the Fugitive Slave Law, were sympathetic to the plight of fugitives, and reported favorably on the activities of the UGRR, remained unwaveringly committed to the idea that there was little future for blacks in the North and their interests were better served if they went to Liberia. This is reflected in the fact that by the end of the decade the most sympathetic newspaper in Harrisburg took to referring to the black community as "Bassa Cove" (a settlement in Liberia) and regularly berated the community for its "degradation," "profanity," and "low vulgarity," drawn from a population made up "to a great extent of indolent, intemperate, worthless and disorderly persons of both sexes, some of whom are before our magistrates almost every day in the week." Almost simultaneously, the same newspaper carried positive reports of the activities of black Masonic lodges, camp meetings, and churches, as well as annual celebrations to commemorate West Indian emancipation on August 1.[48] It was in the context of such ambivalence and antagonism that black communities throughout southeastern Pennsylvania attempted to establish free spaces for themselves, spaces that were created in large part out of a willingness and commitment to welcome those seeking freedom from slavery.

3. Taking Leave

Fugitive Slaves and the Politics of Slavery

On April 14, 1860, almost one year to the day before the outbreak of the Civil War, Nathan James, a free black, and Alfred Savage, a slave drayman, took a large pine box to the Adams Express Company office in Nashville, Tennessee, and arranged to have it shipped to Hannah Johnson—very likely a fictitious person—in Cincinnati, Ohio c/o Levi Coffin. A letter was also sent to Coffin telling him to call for the box at the local Adams Express office. The box traveled by train to Louisville, Kentucky, where it was transferred by ferry across the Ohio River to Jeffersonville, Indiana, and placed on a train for Seymour, Indiana, where it was to be transferred to the Cincinnati-bound train. At Seymour the box was rather unceremoniously thrown onto the platform. The impact caused the box to shatter and out fell a black man, Aleck, who by that time had been in the box for fourteen hours without food or drink.

Aleck was taken into custody, sent off to jail in Louisville, and later returned to Nashville courtesy of the Adams Express Com-

Before it was presented as part of the Brose Lectures, an earlier version of this chapter was given as the Elsa Goviea Memorial Lecture at the University of the West Indies, Mona, Jamaica in 2007.

pany. It turned out that Aleck's owner had been on his trail soon after he failed to show up for work at McClure & Buck, a tin manufacturer, and had wired ahead to the authorities in Louisville asking them to be on the lookout for a slave trying to escape by train. The escape caused considerable excitement locally. The reconfigured box was also returned to Nashville and put on display at the Adams Express office, where men and boys took turns climbing into it and local wags tried their hand at doggerel to commemorate the event.

What do we know of the individuals involved? Nathan James, fifty-one, was born in Virginia. Some reports describe him as a free black, others a "free mulatto." Alf Savage was a slave of his father, who had hired him out on an annual basis since 1845. Aleck was a sheet-metal worker. Also a party to the escape attempt was an unnamed "white man," whose involvement only added to the mystery. Within a week of his return to Nashville, Aleck was brought before Magistrate's Court in an effort to determine who was involved in the plot. The evidence suggests that James and Aleck were members of the same Methodist Episcopal Church. Aleck testified that he had met the white man several times at Alf Savage's. It was the white man who had suggested he escape and who had offered to help him. Before agreeing, Aleck consulted James, who confirmed that the white man, whom he knew, could do the job. Aleck agreed to pay him $60 and, in addition, handed over his silver watch to cover the cost of the escape. The white man procured the box and had it sent to James's home, where Aleck was crated. According to Aleck, the white man had accompanied the crate, periodically checking to make sure he was alive, but disappeared from the train once the plot unraveled in Seymour.

Following the hearing, Savage was sentenced to receive fifteen lashes. James was bound over to appear at the next court session, where it was discovered that he was not free but was in fact a slave who had escaped from Virginia and settled in Nashville some years earlier. He was sentenced to serve time in prison, but the length of his sentence is unknown. At this point the trail goes cold because under Tennessee law slaves could be tried only in police courts, which unfortunately kept no records of their proceedings. Aleck was returned to his master.[1]

Not surprisingly, local and regional newspapers thought they saw the hand of the UGRR in the plot. The connections between James, for all intents and purposes a freeman; Savage, who for years had hired himself out and so lived in a state of quasi-freedom; Aleck, the skilled slave; and the mysterious white man, who was assumed to be a northerner, plus the fact that a box was used (reminiscent of the successful escape of Henry "Box" Brown from Richmond, Virginia, in 1848, which still haunted slaveholders) and the box was addressed to Levi Coffin, the well-known leader of the UGRR in the Cincinnati area, suggest that speculation about the involvement of the UGRR was not too far-fetched. Escapes such as Aleck's demonstrated a degree of planning and coordination and a level of sophistication that deeply troubled local authorities. It pointed to the continued vulnerability of slave property; the willingness of slaves to gamble on and, where necessary, to use their limited resources to pay for attempts to reach freedom; the participation of free blacks, who for many represented the Achilles' heel of the system; and the difficulty of keeping tabs on the many northern whites who moved freely in and out of the Nashville area. But much of the difficulty, many recognized, was also self-imposed: the system's inability to control slaves who, like Aleck and Alf Savage, moved about relatively freely in the city and attended church with free blacks and other slaves, thus carving out spaces of relative freedom for themselves.

It was more than paranoia that drove slaveholders to see the work of the UGRR and sympathetic organizations and individuals behind slave escapes. Slaves planning to flee were sometimes aided by outsiders and local supporters, many of them white. In late 1853 Francis Moss, twenty-nine years old and reputed to be a Canadian, was caught running off three slaves—Charles, Phillis, and Jesse—from Boonville, Missouri. Moss was quickly tried and sentenced to five years in the state penitentiary. The plot thickened when letters from Cincinnati and Macon, Georgia, addressed to Charles were intercepted at the Boonville post office and revealed that he was really Robert Pelham, a free black who, as a local newspaper reported, "suffered himself to be sold, the more readily to succeed in enticing away slaves." If this seemed a little far-fetched, the paper's editor reported that Charles's putative owner, Lofton Windsor, had bought him from Ruben Bartlett, a prominent St. Louis slave trader. Also found on Charles were notes in his own handwriting showing possible routes and distances between Alton, Illinois, and Detroit. As if to add mystery to what was already an unusual case, the letters to Charles mentioned a "Lord Hamilton," which the editor assumed was a reference to Moss. The mystery did not end there. Four years later Moss's parents, Elizabeth and John Rowe, wrote the governor of Missouri from Alton, pleading for a pardon of their "unfortunate son, known in the State Prison of Missouri as Francis Moss."[2]

Hugh Hazlett, a thirty-one-year-old white man who had lived on the Eastern Shore of Maryland for about three years, was caught in 1858 north of Greensboro, in Caroline County, with seven fugitive slaves from Dorchester County on their way to Delaware and Philadelphia. Hazlett was sentenced to forty-four years, six months, and nine days by Dorchester County courts. The unusually lengthy and exact sentence suggests that local authorities were determined to make an example of Hazlett.[3] Much of the uncertainty and suspicion surrounding those involved in the activities of the UGRR in the South centered on northern whites who used their involvement in legitimate business as a cover for their activities. Itinerant peddlers from the North, a common sight on southern roads, were particularly suspect. In June 1854 Thomas Brown, an itinerant peddler, was arrested in Indiana for aiding a female slave and her two children escape from Morganfield, Union County, Kentucky. Brown, aged sixty, and his wife had moved from Cincinnati, where it was rumored he had been involved in UGRR activities, to Henderson, Kentucky, in the spring of 1850. Mrs. Brown opened a millinery store in Henderson, and her husband sold her wares from his wagon both in Kentucky and across the river in Indiana. Brown came under suspicion at a time when a number of slaves had escaped from the area. He was tried and sentenced to the state penitentiary but was pardoned after three years, partly because of his advanced age and ill health.[4]

Those who, as one Richmond editor put it, came sometimes in the "shape of Yankee preachers" and other times as "Yankee lecturers," spewing their "poisonous sentiments," also caused considerable alarm—none more so than Calvin Fairbank, an Oberlin College–trained minister. Fairbank was caught helping Tamar, a slave, escape from Louisville, Kentucky, when the buggy on which they were traveling broke down in Jeffersonville, Indiana. Although the slave managed to elude the authorities, Fairbank was brought back to Louisville, tried, and sentenced. This was Fairbank's second brush with the law. In 1844 he and his partner, Delia Webster, had been convicted and sentenced for helping Lewis Hayden escape, she to two years, he to fifteen years in prison. Fairbank was pardoned after four years. This time he would languish in the state penitentiary until pardoned in 1864 as the Civil War drew to a close.[5]

Northern free blacks also played a pivotal role in getting slaves out of the South. Four years before Nathan James was involved in helping Aleck escape from Nashville, James Peck, a twenty-five-year-old cook on board the steamship *Ella*, which sailed between Nashville and Cincinnati, was charged with helping a slave named Jack flee the city. Peck, who was born in Pittsburgh, Pennsylvania, and lived in Cincinnati, had made three previous trips to Nashville. It seems that he and Mary Gibbs, a chambermaid on the ship who was also from Cincinnati, had slipped Jack on board just before the ship set sail. Jack was not discovered until the ship neared Hawesville, Kentucky. The captain had the three arrested and confined in a local prison. The case against Gibbs was dropped when she agreed to turn state's witness. Peck was convicted of harboring a slave and sentenced to seven years in the state penitentiary.[6]

Free blacks who lived in the South were also suspected of involvement in the UGRR. When thirty slaves escaped from Cambridge, Maryland, one night, the local authorities fixed their suspicion on the Reverend Samuel Green, a free black preacher. Once it became apparent that the slaves had all used the same route out of slavery, a route that passed directly in front of Green's home, authorities were convinced of his involvement. They raided his home, where they found a copy of Harriet Beecher Stowe's *Uncle Tom's Cabin*, a map of Canada, train schedules and routes to the North, and a letter from his son, a former slave who had escaped earlier and was then living in Canada, "detailing the pleasant trip he had, the number of friends he met with on the way, with plenty to eat and drink" and telling his father to let two slaves know that it was time to leave. The two slaves, as it turned out, were among the thirty who passed outside Green's house on their way north. It was also discovered that Green had recently visited Canada. The authorities were ultimately unable to tie Green to the escape, but they were determined to punish him nonetheless. He was convicted under the terms of an obscure 1841 law that banned free blacks from possessing abolitionist literature and sentenced to ten years in the state penitentiary.[7]

In Louisville, Kentucky, the authorities were not similarly able to punish a suspected UGRR agent. Although they kept a close watch on James Cunningham, a prominent black musician who for years had provided entertainment on passenger boats traveling the Ohio River (whom one local newspaper sarcastically referred to as "the well-known Professor of the polite art of dancing"), they were unable to prove his involvement in the effort to help slaves escape. For three years the local police suspected him of running off slaves but were unable to lay "ropes on him." His home, like Rev. Green's, was raided, and the police found letters from Calvin Fairbank as well as the clothes of slaves who had previously gone missing. They also suspected that he was involved with Shadrach Henderson, who had escaped to Canada in late 1853 and then returned to the Louisville area to encourage slaves to escape. But none of this was enough to charge him with a crime. When, in April 1854, Cunningham came to court on another matter, the authorities tried unsuccessfully to intimidate him into admitting complicity in the escape of a number of local slaves. Frustrated, all the magistrate could do was release him on bail of $500 to be on good behavior for one year. The combined efforts of the police and the courts proved totally unavailing, as Cunningham, with the help of allies in Louisville and across the river in New Albany, Indiana, continued to help slaves escape.[8]

Slaves were also aided by other African American outsiders, including some former slaves. The activities of Harriet Tubman are now legendary, but there were many other examples of former slaves returning south to aid slaves to escape. In January 1853 Richard Neal was picked up at his workplace in Philadelphia and charged with returning to Maryland to entice his family and other slaves to escape. Neal had bought his freedom from Isaac Mayo, who ironically was the commodore of the African Squadron stationed on the West Coast of Africa to interdict the illegal slave trade. Apparently, Neal had returned a number of times to Anne Arundel County, where he not only managed to get out his wife and children, who were owned by Mayo, but also other slaves from neighboring plantations. Mayo, who was about to set sail for Africa, had Neal arrested for abducting his slaves and, using his political clout, had the governor of Maryland request the extradition of Neal as a fugitive from justice. Neal was handed over to Mayo and a Maryland policeman following a brief hearing. But friends and members of the local abolition society obtained a writ of habeas corpus from the Pennsylvania Supreme Court, which in the end freed Neal.[9]

The system sometimes had a difficult time identifying the race of subversive outsiders. In May 1860 Louisville, Kentucky, police arrested A. H. Scott and John Henry at a local hotel. The two men had been in town almost four weeks. Scott claimed to be a painter from Covington, Kentucky; Henry, described in newspaper accounts as a mulatto, claimed to have escaped from Macon, Georgia. Scott, who at first was thought to be white, turned out to be also a fugitive from Georgia. But what worried the authorities even more was the discovery of daguerreotypes of black men and women in Henry's possession, suggesting that those who were to be abducted had been identified and targeted earlier. Opponents of the system, it appeared, had availed themselves of the most recent technology in their efforts to deny the system the ability to protect itself. But where the prints were made and who provided them remained a mystery. The uncovering of the daguerreotypes was potentially much more significant, the police seemed to think, than the earlier discovery of a book found in the home of Dick Buckner, a free black laborer, listing the names of slaves, many of whom had escaped recently. Buckner had been under surveillance for some time after the escape of a slave woman, Buckner's stepdaughter, and her child in February 1858. Along with the book, police found several railway tickets, a carpetbag of clothes, and a Bible belonging to Harrison Laville, who had fled with his wife to Canada earlier, as well as a letter from J. Wesley Ray, a fugitive slave from Shelby County, Kentucky, now living in Chatham, Canada, thanking Buckner for sending him a cloak. Buckner was described in newspaper accounts as an active secret agent of the Republican Party and a conductor on the UGRR, which a local newspaper editor viewed as politically one and the same. He was sentenced to two years in the state penitentiary.[10]

All the evidence suggests that outsiders such as Scott and Henry did not act alone. When the police raided James Cunningham's house they found clothes belonging to Tamar, who had fled with Calvin Fairbank, as well as letters from Fairbank. They also found evidence that Cunningham was involved with Shadrach Henderson who, according to a Cincinnati newspaper report, had returned "to assist some colored friends off by the underground line."[11] But few locals suspected of collusion were brought to heel, and when they were, the network of which they were a part survived their incarceration.

Slaves such as Alf Savage who helped other slaves escape yet chose to remain in slavery were an integral part of this network. Following a rash of escapes from Norfolk, Virginia, William Sales, a drayman, was arrested for aiding six slaves to escape on a steamer. In the eyes of one observer there was no doubt that there existed "a society among the slaves at Norfolk, which is organized for the purpose of aiding negroes in escaping from their owners." One failure did not dissuade others from trying to escape. A few days after Sales was taken into custody, fifteen slaves took flight on board an unknown ship. A steamer was hired to pursue them as far as New Bedford, Massachusetts. All along the divide between freedom and slavery fugitives found aid and comfort among slaves who chose to stay behind. For four years, Arnold Gragston, a slave in Mason County, Kentucky, ferried slaves across the Ohio River to Ripley, Ohio, before deciding in the middle of the Civil War to leave himself.[12]

In spite of these legitimate concerns about outside and inside interference with their property, slaveholders nonetheless underestimated the determination and ability of slaves to plan and execute their own escapes. Days before the adoption of the Fugitive Slave Law an advertisement appeared in a Lynchburg, Virginia, newspaper announcing the escape of Joe and Henry from their master in Greensboro, North Carolina, and offering a reward of $500. The owner worried that the slaves may have already left the state or were preparing to do so. He was also unsure if Joe and Henry had acted on their own or were being aided by "abolitionists or free negroes," "seducers or harborers," who, one suspects, were, at least in the eyes of this master, one and the same. Although the master could not bring himself to openly admit it, the decision to leave and how and where to go may very well have been made by Joe and Henry acting on their own initiative or with the aid of family or friends. In another instance, John Smith fled his owner, Samuel Roberts of Baltimore County, Maryland, in April 1854 and promptly changed his name to William Hog once he got to Pennsylvania. Roberts knew from experience that his former slave was likely heading for Pennsylvania. His suspicions were confirmed in the records of the Philadelphia Vigilance Committee. William Still, the committee's secretary, who kept meticulous notes on all those the committee assisted, recorded that Hog walked to Columbia, Pennsylvania, and from there caught a train to Philadelphia.[13] All the evidence suggests that, like Joe and Henry, Hog planned and executed his escape without the aid of others until he crossed into freedom, where, Still implied, he was assisted to get to Philadelphia.

Slaves also left in groups, sometimes made up of family members and other times comprised of friends. These "stampedes" were frequent occurrences and caused considerable stir locally. Peter and his wife Cassa, for example, led their family of fourteen from Montgomery County, Maryland, to Pennsylvania in August 1852. Two months later newspapers in the area announced the escape of another group of sixteen. There are many recorded group escapes from this part of Maryland and other areas of the Upper South throughout the 1850s, including the eight who escaped in May 1856, taking with them $300 worth of silks, dresses, and jewelry. The goods were recovered in Pennsylvania but not the slaves. The implication is that the slaves may have deliberately used the stolen goods as a way to throw slave hunters off their trail. But why they decided to abandon the booty once they got to free territory is unclear.[14] Twenty one fugitives arrived in Philadelphia by boat from Norfolk in November 1855. A few days later Still recorded the arrival of eleven from Chestertown, Maryland.[15]

These patterns of escape are replicated throughout the decade along all sections of the Border States from Virginia to Missouri. Border State slaveholders wrestled with ways to calculate and control their financial losses. Just south of the Pennsylvania state line, a Hagerstown, Maryland, newspaper estimated that some slaveholders in the area had lost $50,000, some $75,000, and others even $100,000 worth of slaves in "a comparatively recent period."[16] In October 1853, James Armstrong escaped from his master, James Rudd, a Louisville slaveholder of some means. It cost Rudd $92.50 to have Armstrong recaptured, which suggests that he was taken close to the northern bank of the Ohio River. Two months later Armstrong went on the lam again. This time he put some distance between himself and his master but again was recaptured. Armstrong's second escape cost Rudd $27.70 in jail fees and $250 in payment to a slave catcher. Three months later Rudd sold his recalcitrant slave for $1,600, a handsome profit by any measure.[17] For a slave, the cost of a failed escape was many times permanent separation from family, friends, and the place one knew, but, then, one suspects those costs had been factored into Armstrong's escape plans.

Some slaveholders were at a loss to explain why their slaves would choose to leave the place they knew and the comforts of home and family for either the "bleak hills and cold climate of Canada, or . . . the purlieus of some large city or town in this country," as one newspaper editor graphically put it, "to drag out a miserable existence among the hordes of debased and squalid creatures who infest those places, and furnish the Penitentiaries and Almshouses with their annual compliment of inmates, or the Pestilence with its first victims."[18] Like Joe and Henry's North Carolina master, they could not explain why slaves would so "suddenly and mysteriously disappear without any cause." Others thought they knew the reason. One Norfolk editor, a slaveholder himself, insisted it was because too much leniency was shown slaves and free blacks. Masters, he warned, had to be more vigilant if they were ever to put a stop to these frequent escapes.[19]

The frequent departure of slaves and the activities of the network that sometimes assisted them raised questions about the methods employed in first planning and then executing escapes. In Louisville and all along the length of the Ohio River, as well as elsewhere in the Upper South, the authorities tried to disrupt the movement through a combination of extensive police surveillance and carefully crafted laws that attempted to plug holes in the many ways slaves could cross into free territory. In Kentucky, ferrymen were held liable for any slave who escaped on their boats, and it became illegal for locals to simply tie up their skiffs on the bank of the Ohio River. Louisville created an extensive policing system over the years. By the mid-1850s there was a police chief, a night police division, and several detectives. There were also watchmen and sheriffs. These were complemented by a wide array of sentries, captains, and clerks on steamers, and neighborhood informants, all of whom had the power to stop and apprehend suspects. At the back of it all was a slew of local ordinances requiring ferrymen under pain of fines to ensure that only those African Americans with the requisite documents were allowed on board their boats and a system of courts, both police and circuit, in which cases were adjudicated.[20]

Although over the years the slave system had developed fairly flexible mechanisms to stem the tide of escapes, slaveholders remained deeply frustrated by their inability to identify exactly who was involved and what means were employed to destabilize the system. The frustration is palpable in the warning to other masters from Joe and Henry's North Carolina owner that something had to be done, and done quickly, by "all persons opposed to negro-stealing." If, as he warned, "the vigilance of the country is not aroused quickly to detect their plans, and arrest and convict negro-stealers, my loss of two such valuable slaves, will be what others may soon expect." Slaveholders took such warnings to heart. Wherever they were most vulnerable they created defensive organizations to protect their interests. In the wake of a rising number of escapes from Mason, Bracken, Pendleton, and Boone counties along the Ohio River in Kentucky—what one local newspaper called a "leave-taking fever"—area slaveholders formed an association at a meeting in Minerva in November 1852 to address the problem. The association made an inventory of members' slaves, established what it called a "pursuing committee" to respond promptly to escapes, created a permanent fund to cover the cost of recaptures, and offered rewards of $300 to anyone in a free state who captured a runaway. Similar organizations appeared periodically along the Mississippi River in Missouri, from Cape Girardeau in the south to Hannibal and Palmyra in the north. An association was formed in Marion County, home of the latter two towns, a few months after the meeting in Minerva. It set up a patrol to detect abolitionist and their agents' meddling as well as to track down fugitives. A later meeting of slaveholders from Marion County and neighboring Ralls County established a committee of six from each county to pursue slaves and established a fund to defray the cost associated with the recapture of slaves who ran away from members. In October 1856 the overwhelming majority of slaveholders in the Twenty-third District of Davidson County, along the Cumberland River in Tennessee, came together to form an organization to protect themselves against slave incendiarists and runaways.[21]

But, as we have seen in the written communication between Rev. Green and his son, opponents of the slave system had devised ways to circumvent such restrictions. Years earlier the issue of how to limit communications between slaves in Richmond and former slaves and free blacks in the North came to a head when Robert Ryland, white pastor of the First African Church, discovered that escaped slaves had been writing "to their former comrades, here, detailing the manner of their escape, and proposing to them facilities and information for the same experiment." Rather than act as a policeman and open and read the letters sent to members of his congregation, Ryland announced, much to the annoyance of many in the city, that, in the future, he would simply not "deliver any letters from the North without a personal acquaintance with and full confidence in the recipient." It is not clear if Ryland's approach solved the problems in his church. The fact that, throughout the 1850s, there were frequent calls for slaveholders to read all letters addressed to slaves suggests that the problem defied resolution by the authorities.[22]

It was generally assumed by advocates of the slave system, even when the evidence suggested otherwise, that fugitive slaves could not have acted on their own. As a result, slaveholders made every effort to stop the bleeding by first trying to identify the subversives in their midst and then devising ways to bring them to heel. The conviction that there were, besides known collusionists such as Nathan James, Calvin Fairbank, Thomas Brown, and James Peck, many more unnamed men and women, white and black, operating in their communities kept slaveholders awake at night. All who assisted the slaves to escape, whether they were other slaves, free blacks, or whites, were automatically considered members of the UGRR, that "infernal route in our midst," as one frustrated editor described it. Any man "who was mean enough to hire himself to an Abolitionist society to persuade slaves to leave comfortable homes and kind masters, under the pretence of securing to them a freedom they are not capable of appreciating or enjoying," was simply a scoundrel who sold his soul for a mere pittance.[23]

Of one thing slaveholders were sure: slaves escaped with alarming frequency. The number of advertisements for runaways provides some measure of the problem. But it is not always easy to determine which slaves set out to reach the North, which, as in the case of Nathan James chose to move to another slave state, or which simply moved to another part of the state to be near family.[24] Advertisements do provide some clues, but they are far from definitive. We should take at their word those masters who made it clear they believed their slaves were heading for the North. Joe and Henry's North Carolina master was pretty certain where his valuable slaves were heading, and in this he was not alone. In taking pains to point out what the slaves took, including sometimes many items of clothing, horses, and arms, others implied, if they did not say explicitly, that the fugitives were determined to reach free territory. The establishment of differential rewards depending on how far from home a slave was captured is another indication that masters kept open the possibility that their slaves would reach freedom.

As we have seen, masters and local authorities in the Upper South created a wide-ranging and sometimes sophisticated posse system to intercept fugitives before they reached freedom and to retake them if they did. When Stephen Pembroke, brother of the prominent black minister and former Maryland slave, J. W. C. Pennington, and his two sons fled Maryland in 1854, their master trailed them all the way to New York City, where they were captured and then returned home. In 1855 John Pope, sheriff of Frederick, Maryland, near to where the Pembrokes were slaves, wrote his counterpart in Montreal proposing cooperation in retaking fugitives who had reached Canada. Someone there would be hired to entice former slaves to come close to the border, where Pope or his men could seize them. Pope had already established what he called a "corps of spies" along the border between Maryland and Pennsylvania that he claimed had some success in cutting off escape routes. He now needed to expand his operation. Pope was publicly ridiculed in the northern press, and it is not clear what if any success he had in persuading northern and Canadian officials to join his effort.[25]

These personal and for-profit efforts were supplemented and reinforced by official state action. Numerous laws were passed, if they were not always enforced, by each of the Border States to cope with the problem. And, during the 1850s, Virginia passed a series of laws all of which aimed at either facilitating the recovery or, as they said, the protection of slave property and all of which provided inducements for free blacks to immigrate to Liberia. The centerpiece was an 1856 law "providing additional protection for slave property of citizens of the commonwealth," under which all vessels trading in the Chesapeake, and on the Potomac and Rappahannock rivers were subject to inspection by patrol boats. Slave escapes by boat had long troubled authorities in Virginia and Maryland, and it was well known that northern abolitionist organizations such as the Philadelphia Vigilance Committee offered payments to captains to conceal slaves on board their ships and ferry them to freedom. The additional protection, it was hoped, would close off one avenue of escape by forcing ship captains and crews, who were subject to heavy fines and imprisonment if slaves were found on their vessels, to desist.[26]

The courts lay at the heart of the southern system to protect slave property. Under the terms of the 1856 Virginia law, communities along the Chesapeake were authorized to establish courts where they did not already exist to try those who were caught with slaves on board their ships. Other local courts played a vital role in protecting slave property. As in the Border States, in Virginia, mayor's courts were the first line of defense. Almost daily during the last three months of 1852, for example, the Richmond Mayor's Court handled cases of runaways and recaptures, as well as reports of free blacks caught without a pass or the right sort of pass. There were twenty-eight cases of slave escapes and recaptures and thirty-seven instances of free blacks being brought to court for being in the city illegally. The sheer volume of cases gives the impression of a highly efficient and vigilant legal system at work. But the frequency of reports also carries a tale of slave disquiet and resistance. Reports are also silent on the number of slaves who may have successfully eluded the reach of the law. In spite of these efforts, restrictions on black testimony in cases involving whites undermined the efficiency of the courts as an instrument of control. Had the "white man" involved in Aleck's escape from Nashville been caught, Aleck could not have testified against him, which increased the likelihood that the white man would have escaped the clutches of the law unless another white person could be found to testify against him. Periodically, there were calls for state legislatures in the Slave States to allow blacks to testify against whites accused of meddling with slaves, especially if the accused whites were from a free state.[27] But nothing ever came of such suggestions, because, one suspects, had they been implemented, it would have been impossible to limit testimony to only certain cases.

If, in the end, all these protective measures were unsuccessful, others had to be devised and deployed. In the Virginia legislature a select committee had declared as an undeniable fact that the emissaries of the UGRR had "penetrated into the very heart of the slave holding states, and aided the escape of slaves whom they seduced from the service of their owners." One response to such depredations was a boycott of northern goods. As one newspaper editor observed, because the South fed and clothed the North it could "stop every loom in Old England and New England, we can transfer the capital, and the machinery, and the operatives employed in the purchase and manufacture of cotton to the South." He was not calling for an immediate boycott, but if New England did not mend its ways and put a break on the activities of abolitionists, things might, he threatened, eventually come to that.[28] The suggestion raised serious constitutional issues, which the editor was not willing to take to their logical conclusion but which in the end went to the heart of the slogan "Cotton is King" and spoke to the hopes of those who believed that the South could go its own way.

As part of the broader political debate between the sections, southern newspapers never missed an opportunity to print accounts of former slaves who had decided against a life of freedom and wished to return to slavery. One woman, formerly of Harpers Ferry, Virginia, wrote her former master comparing the old place favorably to Canada, where there was nothing, she was reported to have said, but "hard times and bad darkies." While abolitionists willingly aided fugitives to get to Canada, one newspaper observed, they did nothing to ensure their survival there. As a result, there was considerable destitution among the fugitives, many of whom crossed the river to Detroit in the winter to "beg and steal." This was no freedom other than a "freedom to starve and die." Many who had left Virginia, the editor comforted his readers, would now be happy to renounce the freedom of an unfeeling and uncaring North to return to the comforts and security they once knew in the South.[29] Furthermore, many slavery apologists believed, those fugitives from slavery who chose to settle in a northern state rather than go on to Canada created a unique set of problems for their host communities, either because they showed signs of degeneracy and so became wards of the state or because they frequently married local white women, violating all established rules of decency. These marriages between "delicate white girls . . . [and] the rough hewn woolly-headed African" only encouraged amalgamation. Yet those who promoted the UGRR seemed oblivious to the consequences of their actions. "Let the Underground go ahead," one editor warned. "The colored gentleman will be very glad to go home with the officers and marry into their families."[30] A more brazen and heavy-handed play on racial sensibilities is hard to find.

In spite of the best efforts of slaveholders and southern municipal authorities, slaves continued to escape. At times when the numbers of escapes spiked, as they frequently did over the course of the 1850s, slaveholders did what they could to protect their property. Some moved or sold their slaves further south. Others called on state governments to do something to curtail the activities of those involved in enticing slaves to escape. In less than two years in the early 1850s nine slaves from the small community of Berlin in Worcester County on the Eastern Shore of Maryland fled north, among them Sarah Airs, who left just before Christmas 1853, and her husband Peter Johnson, who in a coordinated effort followed ten months later. This could not in any way be considered a significant number given that there were over 3,000 slaves in Worcester County in 1850. Nonetheless, the escapes troubled slaveholders, who saw them as a prelude to wider slave disturbances. As a result, two of them, Curtis Jacobs and his father-in-law, William Holland, decided in June 1856 to put some distance between their slaves and those who would persuade them to leave, an approach that would be followed more systematically by slaveholders during the Civil War. They transferred thirty-eight "head of negroes," as Jacobs put it, to Alabama, where they were to be leased out to local slaveholders. Evidently, Jacobs had intercepted letters from "paid abolitionists" mailed from Cold Spring, New York, and from Canada West informing his slaves that wagons and mules had been procured to take them out, rather auspiciously, on July 4.

Jacobs spoke for other slaveholders on the Eastern Shore, even if they did not adopt his solution, when he called for united action in the face of the continued loss of property and the growing danger of slave revolts. The villains of the piece as far as Jacobs was concerned were the large number of free blacks in the state, who by their very presence set a bad example to the slaves, and whites from outside who participated in and financed the activities of the UGRR. "The large number of free negroes around us," he confided to his diary, "and I am sorry to say so but it is true, that we have also in our white population many who put them up to this plot, together with several regular abolitionists who have been traveling amongst us under the pretence of other business."[31]

Jacobs had long been a strident voice for more stringent controls on the free black population. He was chair of the Committee on the Free Black Population set up by the state constitutional convention in 1851. Behind the committee's mandate lay the assumption that the free black population was fast becoming an intractable if not menacing problem. The committee sought to determine the size of the population and how many had been colonized in Africa since 1831, as well as recommend ways to deal with the problem. Concerned that the free black population would outstrip the white population in "a few years," the committee recommended that no free black be allowed to purchase real estate after the adoption of the constitution, that there be no future emancipation unless the freed person leave the state within 30 days, and that no free black be allowed to settle in the state in the future.[32]

As far as Jacobs was concerned, the link between the growth of the free black population and the instability of the slave system was indisputable. The situation in Worcester County drove the point home. In 1790 there was one free black to every forty-three whites; by 1850 the ratio stood at one to three and a half. Not only was the number of free blacks as a percentage of the white population higher in Maryland than in any other state, in Jacobs's home county the percentage was even higher.[33] Nothing came of Jacobs's committee recommendations. They were allowed to languish until the upsurge of escapes from the Eastern Shore in 1858 gave them new life. Under the influence of Jacobs, those in the area who had lost slaves took the initiative to call a series of local meetings that culminated in a statewide Slaveholders Convention held in Baltimore that year. A preliminary meeting in Worcester County adopted a series of resolutions that called for the establishment of a system of payment for those who exposed tampering with slaves, the discontinuation of the practice of slave hiring, a ban on issuing passes to slaves, a willingness to abandon all attempts by citizens of the state to retake fugitive slaves who had fled to another state and instead enter an agreement with the federal government to deliver up all escaped slaves exactly as the 1850 law was meant to operate, the appointment and payment of agents whose jobs it would be to "ferret out" all fugitives, and the adoption of a law requiring all postmasters to "read all letters and other documents addressed to free negroes and slaves."[34]

Even before the convention met in Baltimore there were those who rejected calls for the expulsion of free blacks as wrongheaded, though they agreed that something had to be done with those free blacks they considered useless and dangerous. Although Jacobs was one of the driving forces at the convention, the committee on resolutions made a point of rejecting calls for general removal as both "impolitic and inexpedient" and reiterated what Jacobs saw as a timeworn policy of strengthening the 1831 law that promoted the piecemeal removal of free blacks to Liberia. Jacobs immediately opposed the committee's recommendations. He rejected colonization as a "great humbug," a "fruitless enterprise." The evidence of time was on his side. Free blacks had shown no inclination to go to Africa and much preferred staying in Maryland. As his 1851 committee had shown, only 1,001 had moved to Liberia since 1831, a paltry return on the state colonization society's expenditure to date of $298,000. Refusing to leave the state, what then was to be done with this menace in slavery's midst? Jacobs believed that the state had the power to do with its free black population as it wished. Therefore, it could choose to either expel them or give them the option of choosing a master and going into slavery. Borrowing a page from George Fitzhugh, he declared "I would have all negroes to be slaves in order that all whites may be free."[35]

By the end of the 1850s Jacobs was serving as a member of the state house, where he promoted a bill calling for either the expulsion of free blacks or, if they refused and wished to stay, their reenslavement. That the bill was rejected says something about divisions among slaveholders over the best course to pursue. One western Maryland editor dismissed Jacobs's arguments as a "batch of the most absurd nonsense—the grossest unconstitutionality—and the most barbarous inhumanity that ever emanated from the mind of a cracked-brained mono maniac."[36] There were, opponents reasoned, when they were not openly belittling Jacobs, more than enough laws on the books to control the free black population. But behind this questioning of Jacobs's sanity was a genuine fear that, should the law be implemented, free blacks would choose to leave, and, in so doing, ruin the state's economy.

Some outside observers thought slaveholders acted as if hunting down fugitives were a sport akin to fox hunting. Nothing was further from the truth. As far as slaveholders in the Upper South were concerned, recovering their property was serious business. They felt themselves to be under constant siege from the slaves who, acting individually or sometimes in groups, regularly sought their freedom. There was no way to predict when and where the next attempt to escape would occur. Such unpredictability created a sense of vulnerability and bred deep suspicions among slaveholders, who, try as they may, could not bring themselves to believe that their slaves were acting without the aid of others. Jacobs's was undoubtedly a unique and overexcited imagination, but his obsession with the free black menace reflected many of the concerns of his fellow slaveholders. So, too, did his views about the threat of outside whites. He was also convinced, and said so frequently, that outsiders' activities were financed largely by contributions from British abolitionists. Ways had to be found, therefore, to control the activities of both free blacks and those whites who meddled with the system, the better to curtail escape attempts by the enslaved. Local methods were buttressed by statewide associations and by the political muscle of state and national governments. Yet over the broad sweep of the decade, nothing they did could stem the bleeding totally. Thus, the actions of the slaves reverberated through the political landscape, affecting what local authorities did, relations between states across the slavery divide, and, in times of crisis such as the attempt to recapture a fugitive, the politics of northern communities. Serious questions were raised, for example, about the nature of relations between Maryland and Pennsylvania in the wake of the murder of a slaveholder attempting to retake slaves at Christiana, Pennsylvania, in September 1851. The Christiana incident may have been one of the most dramatic events of the decade, but all along the border between freedom and slavery—at the points of maximum tension—lesser incidents involving fugitive slaves continued to have a profound effect on politics in the years leading up to the Civil War.

Conclusion: Counternarratives

In May 1858, William Connelly, a thirty-year-old former reporter for the Cincinnati *Commercial* announced that he would reveal the workings of the UGRR. It was a startling declaration, the sort of news opponents of the largely secret organization had been seeking for years. Such an exposé from someone who was involved could be the prelude to the dismantling of what many considered the nation's principal domestic enemy, a group responsible for undermining one of the pillars of the liberal democratic state: a form of private property. Not surprisingly, supporters of the UGRR worried about the possible consequences should Connelly expose the details of how the local organization functioned—its methods of operation, its financing, its avenues of communication across the Ohio River, and the people who made it all work. One year earlier, Connelly had hidden Irvin and Angeline Broadhaus, who had fled from Covington, Kentucky, directly across the Ohio River from Cincinnati, in an apartment he rented. The local sheriff got wind of their whereabouts, and when he tried to take them in, Irvin resisted. In the melee, Irvin was fatally wounded and the sheriff injured. The dying Irvin was summarily returned to Covington, along with Angeline, as the law required. Connelly fled town but was captured seven months later in New York City and returned to Cincinnati for trial. At the end of the trial a sympathetic magistrate found Connelly guilty but imposed the most lenient penalty possible: twenty days in prison and a fine of $10. On his release, Connelly was met by an enthusiastic crowd of supporters and paraded through the streets as if to trumpet their defiance of the law. His involvement in the attempted escape of the Broadhauses was celebrated at a public meeting that evening. It is there that he made his promise to lay bare the workings of the UGRR at a meeting that was planned for the following evening at an African American church. It is very likely, however, that Connelly thought better of his promise or was pressured not to say much about what he knew, for he told his audience the next evening little that was revealing. In the end, opponents were disappointed but supporters were relieved that the organization's secrets remained intact.[1]

Contemporaries were intrigued by the UGRR, its secrecy only helping to deepen the mystery surrounding it. By 1850 myths surrounding the operations of the clandestine organization were commonplace. The unexpected and sudden disappearance of slaves from southern towns and plantations was invariably attributed to the presence of white men from outside the area; of free black subversives, whether home grown or imported; or of other slaves who hid runaways and helped get them to safety. Advertisements for runaway slaves echoed these speculations and uncertainties. When fugitives reached free territory, they seemed to disappear in an underground network of safe houses in rural and urban black communities and among white sympathizers. Yet given the significant numbers who were retaken, it is clear slaveholders and their supporters had developed a counternetwork of spies and informants, aided by local, state, and national officials, that helped to ferret out escapees.

Unlike Connelly, Franklin Wilmot, who claimed to be a former operative, did reveal secrets of the UGRR, publishing a pamphlet in 1860 that set out to expose the complex workings of the organization. Nothing is known of Wilmot, but he supposedly became involved with the abolitionist movement at a low point in his life when he was unemployed and deeply in debt. He was persuaded to join by John H. Ratlin, whom he met by chance on a street in Boston and who evidently owned property outside Nashville, Tennessee. Ratlin pointed to the existence of an Aiding and Abetting Society, a secret organization that Wilmot unflatteringly described as being made up of "itinerant backsliding ministers, worn out tract colporteurs, elderly females, and a few cunning-looking negroes." Its members raised money that they used to buy farms and plantations in northern Alabama, Tennessee, and Kentucky, where they set up as slaveholders, using their homes as safe havens for local slaves whom they encouraged to escape. Once the runaways crossed the Ohio River, they were sent to either Toledo or Cleveland, where agents of Canadian abolitionists met them and transported them across Lake Erie. The society also sent agents south, each armed with $1,000, maps, and blank freedom papers with forged signatures of judges that were used to facilitate escapes. These agents, all of whom, he implied, were whites, aided by blacks, were paid $300 for each slave they got safely to Canada. By these means he estimated the Society had run off 3,000 slaves between 1856 and 1858. Wilmot himself was offered $3,000 to get three slaves out of southern Kentucky. This was a lucrative if dangerous business, but Wilmot soon grew tired of what he called bigoted fanatics who were bent on causing strife between "people who should be on terms of amity." He also came to understand the true condition of the slaves, whose "imaginary chains," he insisted, sat "lightly as the golden one on the bosom of beauty." In the South, particularly around New Orleans, he saw slaves who were "happy, contented . . . well fed, as their looks testified, well lodged and not over-tasked." Drawing on a long tradition of defenders of slavery, he reported that their conditions were superior to those of the "half-starved and poorly-paid laborers in the North." Wilmot severed all connections with the Aiding and Abetting Society and its activities after he escaped a riverboat fire that nearly took his life. At the time of the pamphlet's publication Wilmot was living in Canada, where he saw former slaves who failed to exploit the riches of the land, preferring to spend their time in "grog-shops and other scenes of debauchery."[2]

Wilmot's pamphlet was meant to be the authentic voice of a participant, someone who had experienced the exhilaration of bringing slaves out but who, in the end, came to rue his involvement in a movement that threatened the very future of the country. If his claims sound far-fetched, they nonetheless confirmed the views of many on both sides of the dispute over slavery. There was ample evidence, as we have seen, to support the contention that, long before the passage of the 1850 law, organizations such as the Aiding and Abetting Society had been sending whites and blacks into the South disguised as peddlers, colporteurs, and teachers to encourage slaves to escape. The "unnamed white man" was not just a figment of the imagination of those who felt themselves hemmed in and under siege; experience suggested he was real. Wilmot also offered his readers a counternarrative to the accounts of slave escapes that were a staple of the abolitionist movement. Here was a man who had once been an active participant in the struggle against slavery, but who, by going south, was finally exposed to the true workings of a system that provided for the welfare of a people who could not provide for themselves, a people who were happy where they were and who, once exposed to the harsh reality of freedom in a place like Canada, succumbed to depravity and penury.

There were others in the North who endorsed and helped to legitimate Wilmot's claims. A few months earlier, and in the wake of John Brown's raid on Harpers Ferry in October 1859, R. J. Halderman, the editor of the Harrisburg *Patriot & Union*, a Democratic newspaper, informed his readers that he had deciphered the mysteries and clandestine operations of the UGRR. It, not slavery, he told his readers, was the "peculiar institution," a place where, he asserted sarcastically, "a certain class of philanthropists makes a practical application of their love of the colored race." Its agents, like burglars, "incendiaries, and other malefactors," were most active at night. They professed a love of the country, its laws and its constitution, and saw themselves as law-abiding citizens, all the while secretly violating those very laws. Inexplicably, they were impervious to the fact that their actions did more harm than good to those they professed to help. Taking a cue from Bunyan's *Pilgrim's Progress*, Halderman indicted those involved in the movement for removing slaves from the "station of Contentment," running them through the "region of mock philanthropy" before depositing them in the land of "Misery." All of this was unnecessary and counterproductive, for slaves were happy where they were. "Sambo is a gay careless darkey," he claimed knowingly, someone who was well cared for with "plenty to eat, plenty to wear, not overworked, and never knew what want was." Along come a few misguided philanthropists who think they know what is best for the slaves and persuade them that "freedom is a fine thing." Ignoring what is in their best interest, slaves take the bait, leave their happy homes, and are warmly received by their new friends, who see them on their way to a new life in Canada or somewhere "within the States, where Abolition philanthropy disseminates an atmosphere of liberty." Once they have put distance between themselves and their master, however, their new friends promptly abandon them, ignoring their needs at a time when they are most vulnerable. In this situation there is now no one to care for their needs, "no master to think" for them. As a result, they become "lazy, idle, worthless vagabond[s] avoided by the very men who transported [them] to freedom." Aware of their own inferiority, they grow "reckless, drone out a useless, pilfering existence, or repose [their] sturdy limbs in the cell or a prison." In turn, the masters they left behind, sensitive to the possibility of other losses, move their remaining slaves further south, out of reach of the agents of the UGRR, to a place where life is much harsher. This, as we have seen, was exactly Curtis Jacobs's argument and the solution he adopted to address the problem of outside interference with his Maryland property. As a consequence of the activities of the UGRR, both masters and slaves suffered, Halderman concluded; the masters were "brought vexation and insecurity," the slaves either "misery at the North or hard labor at the South." Yet in the end Halderman was forced to concede that the UGRR was doing a thriving business locally.[3]

To opponents of the UGRR, Halderman's was a pretty conventional picture of recklessness and abandonment, of the open violation of laws, of political subterfuge that endangered the federal compact, an agreement that had kept the country together nearly seven decades—and, remarkably, all in aid of a people who were incapable of appreciating such assistance or even needed such help. Were it not for the agents of the UGRR, slaves would be content to stay where they were. After all, they were provided for by their masters. But the runaways whom William Still interviewed in his Philadelphia office and the vast number of advertisements offering rewards for the return of slaves published in southern newspapers tell a different story. The enslaved left whenever an opportunity presented itself. Many knew where they were going and had thought long and hard before leaving. Some left to avoid punishment or sale, others because masters had broken agreements, and still others to reconnect with family members who had escaped earlier. They were well aware of what they were doing and the consequences of their actions. They sought freedom and in doing so knew of its costs to their former masters. As Jackson Whitney wrote his former master from Canada in May 1859, he had decided "to take [his] feet feel for Canada, and let your conscience feel in your pocket."[4] But whatever the specific reasons for leaving, collectively their actions were informed by what E. P. Thompson has called a "general notion" of rights and a passionate desire for freedom.[5] Still and other members of the Philadelphia Vigilance Committee who met and interviewed those seeking freedom could not but be impressed by the depth of their commitment to escape slavery, the "ingenious stratagems" they employed, the "imminent perils" they faced, and the "intense bodily suffering through which they passed."[6] The initiative, the runaways made clear, was a far cry from the picture painted by Halderman. "Sambo" was neither lazy nor content.

As Halderman knew, black communities like those in southeast Pennsylvania were magnets for the enslaved fleeing Virginia, Maryland, and Delaware. Hundreds settled in these communities and over the years became full members of them, participating actively in community institutions. Their arrival kept alive and reinforced contacts across the slavery divide. The rhythms of these communities were oftentimes disrupted, the lives of the new arrivals endangered, and contacts with family and friends left behind in slavery broken, if not severed completely, by efforts to impose the mandates of the 1850 Fugitive Slave Law. In the wake of the law, hundreds of former slaves who had made new lives for themselves in the North relocated with their families, opting for the safety of settlements further north in the United States or in Canada. Many of those who chose to stay where they were paid the ultimate price: within a year numerous fugitives were captured and returned to slavery from southeastern Pennsylvania, usually in the dead of night while the community slept and many times without a hearing as provided for by the law. But those who chose to stay and those who continued to arrive found comfort, support, and protection from these communities in open defiance of the law. Under assault from slaveholders, their agents, and local officials, African Americans and their white supporters found sometimes ingenious ways to thumb their noses at the law and undermine its enforcement. They turned out in sizable numbers at courthouses and commissioners' offices to pay noisy witness to their opposition to the law and, whenever the opportunity presented itself, to abduct suspected fugitives and send them to safety. Courtrooms throughout the North echoed with legal disputations and were frequently transformed into political theaters. They arrived early at hearings, packing the courtrooms with supporters of the accused fugitives. They provided witnesses to the fact that the accused had been living in the community long before the stated date of escape. Those who could not gain entry to courthouses stood clamorous vigil outside. In response, local authorities deployed the full weight of their police forces in an effort to control and intimidate the crowds.

Halderman's view of the workings of the UGRR and the political turmoil its activities caused was influenced in large part by the recent case of Daniel Webster, also known as Daniel Dangerfield, who had been captured in Harrisburg in April 1859 and taken to Philadelphia for a hearing. He was accused of escaping five years earlier from Virginia. Five African Americans, including sixty-six-year-old "Dr." William Jones traveled to Philadelphia as witnesses in support of Webster's claim that he had been living in Harrisburg more than a year before it was claimed he had escaped. Scores of Philadelphia supporters arrived early for the hearing and occupied all of the seats available. When the district attorney tried to clear the hearing room, he met with resistance. A large crowd gathered outside threatened to storm the commissioner's office in support of those inside. Some in the crowd were arrested for disorderly conduct, which, as one observer reported, only "aggravated public feelings." The cramped quarters of the hearing room and the un-relenting protest of counsels for Webster against conditions in the room finally forced the commissioner to transfer proceedings to a larger courtroom nearby. The crowd followed. Webster's support-ers, who included a large number of unidentified black women and prominent white abolitionists—among them Lucretia Mott, Pass-more Williamson, and J. Miller McKim—filled the room. Those who came from Harrisburg to testify in support of Webster were initially locked out of the courtroom but, following a protest by Webster's attorney, were admitted. Black and white supporters who could not gain admittance milled about outside, supervised by a contingent of 300 policemen. The hearing lasted until 5:00

A.M. the following morning, yet the crowd outside, even in bitterly cold temperatures, refused to disperse. When the commissioner ruled in favor of Webster, the crowd was jubilant. A spontaneous street celebration followed. The cheering crowd attached a brace of horses to a chaise and took Webster through the streets in what one reporter described as "the very delirium of joy and triumph." That evening Webster's defense counsels were serenaded at a mass meeting. Back in Harrisburg, large crowds marched on the train station "keeping time with martial music" to welcome Webster home. But he never appeared. Supporters in Philadelphia, fearing an appeal of the commissioner's decision, had taken the precaution of sending him to the safety of Canada.[7]

The case received extensive coverage in newspapers throughout Pennsylvania and was picked up by many in others parts of the North. Questions concerning Webster's seizure and removal to Philadelphia were raised in the state house. Some insisted that the case should have been heard in Harrisburg, but ever since the resignation of Richard McAllister, the unpopular fugitive slave commissioner, six years earlier, federal authorities had been unable to find someone to fill the post. Still, that did not mollify opponents of the law or even those supporters who wondered about the political wisdom of transporting suspected fugitives in manacles to another city for trial. The case roiled the political waters in other ways as well. The Philadelphia meeting to celebrate Webster's release attracted both supporters and opponents of the Fugitive Slave Law, all of them determined to make their views known. One local newspaper reported that the meeting was organized by "ultraabolitionists" and attended by "plenty of negroes . . . carrying a very high head since the late decision in favor of the alleged slave Webster." Members of the local Democratic Party, ardent supporters of the law, attended, as did a "number of Southern medical students" enrolled in the city's medical schools. Interestingly, many of these same students would abandon their training and return home following the election of Lincoln the following year. The meeting was frequently disrupted by shouts and catcalls. But even in this tense situation there were moments of levity. The proceedings were interrupted, particularly at moments of high tension, by someone in the audience imitating a rooster. At one juncture a group described as "Democratic roughs" advanced on the stage in an attempt to silence the speakers and capture the meeting. The police had to be called out before order could be restored and the meeting could continue.[8] The enforcement of the law in the face of the enslaved "making freedom" for themselves and the determination of their supporters to limit the reach of the law had a profound effect on the political debate over the future of slavery.

But the release of Webster also seemed to reenergize those in Harrisburg who had profited from their involvement in the business of returning suspected slaves in ways that had not been seen since Commissioner McAllister's resignation. There were reports of the presence of slave catchers from Virginia and Maryland and their connection to a kidnapping gang centered in adjoining York and Cumberland counties, a gang that had gone to ground temporarily following the successful prosecution of some of its leaders three years earlier. As a result, it was reported that a half dozen fugitives who had lived in town and been employed at local hotels since the early years of the decade had left for Canada. One newspaper pleaded with the city to rid itself of these "mercenary dealers in human flesh and blood . . . the meanest specimens of humanity extant," and suggested that the black community was on the verge of giving them a "warm reception."[9]

One enterprising businessman thought he saw an opportunity to benefit from the publicity surrounding the case. In an advertisement, he claimed that while there may have been a difference of opinion over whether Webster should be returned to slavery in the Old Dominion, there was no such conflict over the excellence of the "Old Dominion Coffee Pot."[10] Halderman may have appreciated the businessman's efforts to increase sales but not his humor. Opposition to the enforcement of the law was serious business. There were people in Pennsylvania and throughout the North committed to the law's demise and by implication the severing of the federal compact. Although he did not say so explicitly, there was another element of the UGRR that worried Halderman: those blacks and whites who went into the South to encourage slaves to escape. If Franklin Wilmot is to be believed, Halderman's worse fears were realized.

Almost four decades later, on the eve of the Jim Crow era, as the country retreated from the promises of Reconstruction, the white sons and daughters of those who had participated in the UGRR came to see the need to protect the legacy of their fathers and mothers. Not surprisingly, their memory of what transpired and what was accomplished was clouded by the fog of time. But it was a legacy of which they were understandably proud. The memory, however, largely excluded the contributions of African Americans, enslaved and free, to the struggle for freedom. In early September 1897 a group of about 100 black and white residents of Harrisburg tried to address that shortcoming: making a pilgrimage to a remote spot four miles northeast of the town of Linglestown, nestled in the closest mountain of the Kittatinny Range, they dedicated monuments to mark the resting place of two former slaves who had escaped to Pennsylvania and were buried there. One, who had died in the early years of the Civil War, carried the iconic name George Washington; the other, known either as Brown or Lewis, chose to commit suicide when agents of his master closed in on him in the early 1850s. They were "two negroes," a report observed, "who preferred to live and die in that lonely spot free men to going back to slavery in the South." The monuments to the fugitive slaves were paid for by Charles Smith, a white medical doctor, who grew up in the area and had known Washington. At the start of the formal ceremonies, an American flag that draped the monuments was removed, the attendees sang "My Country 'Tis of Thee," and a passage from 1 Corinthians, chapter fifteen was read: "But he that is spiritual judgeth all things, yet he himself is judged by no man." These were men, the speakers emphasized, who cherished freedom. W. Justin Carter, one of the principal speakers, said of Brown: "He was wretched and had the wisdom to aspire above his fated circumstances. He had the courage to feel that he was a man and when the glorious chance of freedom fled he took his sacred and ignoble life and threw it back at the God that gave it." Here was a man who had the "glorious attributes of dauntless courage because he had learnt and felt the great and infinite truth, the equality of human rights." These monuments, Carter concluded, would tell "the story of George Washington and the unknown, and hallow the deeds of men whose devotion to justice, equality and truth was bounteously brighter than their day." Carter was followed by the main speaker of the day, William Howard Day, an 1847 Oberlin graduate and former newspaper editor who had come of political age in the trying times of the 1850s. Day had moved to Harrisburg after the war, where he became an active member of the black community and the city and in the early years of the 1890s was elected president of the city school board. Day revisited many of the same themes emphasized by Carter. These men, he declared, "knew how to be free and live and die in the employment of liberty after they had attained it." The memorial tablets, he insisted, were not just for the deceased; they were also for the living. "They write again the history of this land[,] telling us of the past and of the present, when under a re-written Constitution, justice and freedom are guaranteed." They reminded the United States that no longer would one man call another master.[11] Strikingly, neither Carter nor Day saw the need to connect the struggles of Washington and Brown to those confronting African Americans as the nineteenth century came to a close. A hard-earned victory had been won, and that was worth remembering and celebrating.

Notes

INTRODUCTION

1. The original study on which we all depend is William Still's magisterial *The Underground Railroad* (Philadelphia, 1872). The classic study is Wilbur H. Siebert, *The Underground Railroad from Slavery to Freedom* (London, 1898), which spawned a number of examinations of the movement in individual states, many of them by Siebert's students. Much of this work came under scrutiny by Larry Gara, *The Liberty Line: The Legend of the Underground Railroad* (Lexington, Ky., 1961). Recently, a number of studies have reexamined the movement and tried to place it in the context of the wider abolitionist struggle. Among these are Stanley Harrold, *Subversives: Antislavery Community in Washington, D.C., 1828–1865* (Baton Rouge, 2003); Kate Clifford Larson, *Bound for the Promised Land: Harriet Tubman, Portrait of an American Hero* (New York, 2004); Fergus M. Bordewich, *Bound for Canaan: The Underground Railroad and the War for the Soul of America* (New York, 2005); Keith P. Griffler, *Front Line of Freedom: African Americans and the Forging of the Underground Railroad in the Ohio Valley* (Lexington, Ky., 2004); Ann Hegedorn, *Beyond the River: The Untold Story of the Heroes of the Underground Railroad* (New York, 2002); David W. Blight, ed., *Passages to Freedom: The Underground Railroad in History and Memory* (Washington, D.C., 2004); and Pamela A. Peters, *The Underground Railroad in Floyd County, Indiana* (Jefferson, N.C., 2001). Peters's book is one in a flurry of local studies of the UGRR, also including William C. Kashatus, *Just over the Line: Chester County and the Underground Railroad* (University Park, Pa., 2001); Harriet C. Frazier, *Runaways and Freed Missouri Slaves and Those Who Helped Them, 1763–1865*

(Jefferson, N.C., 2004); and J. Blaine Hudson, *Fugitive Slaves and the Underground Railroad in the Kentucky Borderland* (Jefferson, N.C., 2002).

2. Hagerstown *Herald of Freedom*, October 9, 1850.

3. Leigh Fought, *Southern Womanhood and Slavery: A Biography of Louisa S. McCord, 1810–1879* (Columbia, Mo., 2003), 54.

CHAPTER 1

1. H. W. Banks to Dear Friend, New York, February 15, 1853, William M. Buck to Dear Sir, Front Royal, February 1, 1854, Buck Family Papers, University of Virginia, Charlottesville (my thanks to Ervin Jordon for copies of this and other letters from the collection); Thomas Ashby to William M. Buck, Philadelphia, February 28, 1853, C. B. Fristoe to Dear Sir, Front Royal, April 13, 1853, H. H. Kline to William M. Buck, Philadelphia, April 22, 1853, E. W. Massey to William Buck, n.p., May 2, 1853, Buck Family Papers, in Kenneth Stampp, ed., "Records of the Ante-Bellum Southern Plantations from the Revolution through the Civil War" (microform), series J, reel 9; Ellen Eslinger, "Freedom Without Independence: The Story of a Former Slave and Her Family," *Virginia Magazine of History and Biography* 114, no. 2 (2006): 264–66. On Henry Kline, see Thomas P. Slaughter, *Bloody Dawn: The Christiana Riot and Racial Violence in the Antebellum North* (New York, 1991), 52–53, and William Still's letter to the *Voice of the Fugitive*, January 1, 1852, in Black Abolitionists Papers Project (microform) (hereafter cited as BAP), reel 7, 318.

2. For Bibb, see John Blassingame, *Slave Testimony: Two Centuries of Letters, Speeches, Interviews, and Autobiographies* (Baton Rouge, 1977), 50. Harriet Jacobs used a similar ruse. In an effort to lead her owner to think she had escaped to New York City, Jacobs wrote two letters, one to her owner and the other to her grandmother. She had a friend take the letters, which were postdated New York. The one to her grandmother asked that a reply be sent to Boston and not to New York, which she visited frequently. Harriet Jacobs, *Incidents in the Life of a Slave Girl* (1861; repr., New York, 2001), 101–2.

3. Nashville *Union and American*, September 20, 1853; Nashville *True Whig*, February 8, 1854; *Southern Illinoisan*, February 24, 1854.

4. Richmond *Whig*, March 4, 1851, August 3, 1852. For a discussion of literacy among slaves and the employment of free papers by runaways, see John Hope Franklin and Loren Schweninger, *Runaway Slaves: Rebels on the Plantation* (New York, 1999), 118–19, 230–31; Steven Hahn, *A Nation under Our Feet: Black Political Struggles in the Rural South from Slavery to the Great Migration* (Cambridge, Mass., 2003), 42–3; and Janet Duitsman Cornelius, *When I Can Read My Title Clear: Literacy, Slavery, and Religion in the Antebellum South* (Columbia, S.C., 1991), 8–9, 90–93.

5. Nashville *True Whig*, August 2, 12, 26, 29, 1854.

6. Scott Christianson, *Freeing Charles: The Struggle to Free a Slave on the Eve of the*

Civil War (Urbana, Ill., 2010), 25–26; Julius Sherrard Scott III, "The Common Wind: Currents of Afro-American Communication in the Era of the Haitian Revolution" (Ph.D. diss., Duke University, 1986), 114–15. Steven Hahn calls these "channels of slave communication" (*A Nation under Our Feet*, 41). John R. McKivigan, ed., *The Roving Editor or Talks With Slaves in the Southern States, By James Redpath* (1859, repr., University Park, Pa., 1996), 239–41. On a visit to South Carolina during the Revolutionary War, John Adams was stunned by the speed with which news was transmitted among the slaves. He wrote in his diary: "The negroes have a wonderful art of communicating intelligence among themselves; it will run several hundreds of miles in a week or fortnight." See Sidney Kaplan and Emma Nogrady Kaplan, *The Black Presence in the Era of the American Revolution* (Amherst, Mass., 1989), 25.

7. For Jackson's life and activities, see, for example, Chester *Record*, April 25, 1863; Bradford *Review*, March 21, 1863; Bury *Times*, April 18, 1863.

8. Thomas Ashby to William M. Buck, Philadelphia, February 28, 1853, E. W. Massey to William Buck, n.p., May 2, 1853, Buck Family Papers, in Stampp, ed., "Records of the Ante-Bellum Southern Plantations," series J, reel 9. As an example of the very complex and sophisticated method of communication employed by fugitives and their families, see the case of Sally Thomas, a Nashville laundress; her free black son, John, living in Florence, Alabama; and her son Henry, a fugitive slave living in Buffalo, New York. John Hope Franklin and Loren Schweninger, *In Search of the Promised Land: A Slave Family in the Old South* (New York, 2006), 47.

9. Robert Ryland, "Reminiscences of the First African Church, Richmond, VA.," *American Baptist Memorial* 14 (November 1855): 323.

10. For a discussion of changes in the postal system, see Richard R. John, *Spreading the News: The American Postal System from Franklin to Morse* (Cambridge, Mass., 1995), 160–61.

11. John T. Kneebone, "A Breakdown of the Underground Railroad: Captain B. and the Capture of the *Keziah*, 1858," *Virginia Cavalcade* 48, no. 2 (Spring 1999): 78; William Still, *The Underground Railroad* (1872; repr., Chicago, 1970), 251–55, 215, 417–18.

12. Still, *The Underground Railroad*, 298–99, 399–400, 191–205; Christianson, *Freeing Charles*, 27; Blassingame, *Slave Testimony*, 427–29.

13. Easton *Gazette*, August 28, 1858; Still, *The Underground Railroad*, 251–55; Richard Albert Blondo, "Samuel Green: A Black Life in Antebellum Maryland" (M.A. thesis, University of Maryland, 1988), 15–17; Kate Clifford Larson, *Bound for the Promised Land: Harriet Tubman, Portrait of an American Hero* (New York, 2004), 141–43; Jean M. Humez, *Harriet Tubman: The Life and the Life Stories* (Madison, Wisc., 2003), 225; Louisville *Courier*, October 6, 8, 12, 1855, August 28, 29, 31, 1857; Louisville *Journal*, January 19, 20, 21, 1859.

14. Laura Haviland, *A Woman's Life-Work: Labors and Experiences of Laura S. Haviland* (Chicago, 1887), 195; David S. Cecelski, "The Shores of Freedom: The Mar-

itime Underground Railroad in North Carolina, 1800–1861," *North Carolina Historical Review* 71, no. 2 (April 1994): 199–200; Still, *The Underground Railroad*, 30.

15. Pittsburgh *Gazette*, October 5, 1854.

16. Journal C of Station 2 of the UGRR, 1852–1857, BAP, reel 7, 13435, 13481–82, 13488, 13552; Still, *The Underground Railroad*, 317, 323, 410.

17. Still, *The Underground Railroad*, 205, 346–47; BAP, reel 7, 13553.

18. H. W. Banks to Dear Friend, New York, February 15, 1853, Buck Family Papers, University of Virginia, Charlottesville.

19. Blassingame, *Slave Testimony*, 423; Benjamin Drew, *The North-Side View of Slavery* (1856; repr., New York, 1968), 133; Richard S. Newman, "'Lucky to be Born in Pennsylvania': Free Soil, Fugitive Slaves and the Making of Pennsylvania's Anti-Slavery Borderland," *Slavery & Abolition* 32, no. 3 (September 2011): 414. For a discussion of the "free soil principle," see Sue Peabody, *There Are No Slaves in France: The Political Culture of Race and Slavery in the Ancien Regime* (New York, 1996), chap. 1. Philip Troutman argues that escaped slaves created a "covert network of information and knowledge," a "geopolitical literacy." Troutman, "Grapevine in the Slave Market: African American Geopolitical Literacy and the 1841 Creole Revolt," in Walter Johnson, ed., *The Chattel Principle: Internal Slave Trades in the Americas* (New Haven, 2004), 203–4.

20. For a discussion of the effects of Dunmore's proclamation, see Simon Schama, *Rough Crossings: Britain, the Slaves, and the American Revolution* (New York, 2005), chap. 1. W. E. B. Du Bois, *Black Reconstruction in America, 1860–1880* (1935; repr., New York, 1971), 62. Edwin H. Cotes described the leave taking as akin to "sheep jumping over a fence w[h]en one goes the[y] all follow." Quoted in Joseph A. Barome, "The Vigilance Committee of Philadelphia," *Pennsylvania Magazine of History and Biography* 92 (July 1968): 324.

21. Jane Landers, "Southern Passage: The Forgotten Route to Freedom in Florida," in David W. Blight, ed., *Passages to Freedom: The Underground Railroad in History and Memory* (Washington, D.C., 2004), 117; see Jane Landers, *American Creoles in the Age of Revolutions* (Cambridge, Mass., 2010), for more comprehensive coverage. Sean Kelly, "'Mexico in His Head': Slavery and the Texas-Mexico Border, 1810–1860," *Journal of Southern History* 37, no. 3 (Spring 2004): 709.

22. Still, *The Underground Railroad*, 44, 278–79; BAP, reel 7, 13515.

23. Edward D. Jerry and C. Harold Huber, "The *Creole* Affair," *Journal of Negro History* 65, no. 3 (Summer 1980): 206.

24. Falmouth *Post*, June 8, 1855.

25. For Harrison, see Edward B. Rugemer, "Robert Monroe Harrison, British Abolition, Southern Anglophobia and Texas Annexation," *Slavery & Abolition* 28, no. 2 (August 2007): 172, and *The Problem of Emancipation: The Caribbean Roots of the American Civil War* (Baton Rouge, 2008), 185–86; Joe B. Wilkins Jr., "Window of Freedom: The South's Response to the Emancipation of the Slaves in the British

West Indies, 1833–1861" (Ph.D. diss., University of South Carolina, 1977), 117; Harrison to William L. Marcy, Kingston, Jamaica, June 21, July 5, 17, 1855, Despatches from the United States Consul in Kingston, Jamaica, 1796–1906 (microform) (hereafter cited as Despatches), vols. 16 and 17.

26. Falmouth *Post*, June 15, 1855; for Harrison's comments on the connections between the Handy and Lewis case and the visit of William W. Anderson to the United States, see Robert Harrison to W. Marcy, Kingston, April 26, 1853, Despatches, vol. 14.

27. Pittsburgh *Gazette*, May 30, 1853; Pittsburgh *Post*, May 31, 1853; Pittsburgh *Commercial Journal*, May 31, 1853; C. Peter Ripley et al., eds., *Black Abolitionist Papers*, Vol. 4, *The United States, 1847–1858* (Chapel Hill, N.C., 1991), 157–60; Rugemer, *The Problem of Emancipation*, 283–84; R. J. M. Blackett, "Black Pittsburgh's Aid to the Fugitive Slave," *Western Pennsylvania Historical Magazine* 61, no. 2 (April 1978): 131; for information on Adams, see 7th United States Census, Montgomery County, Tenn., and 7th United States Census, Slave Schedules, Montgomery County, Tenn.

28. *Pennsylvania Freeman*, April 10, 1851. Many of the organizers of the meeting would emigrate to Liberia in 1864 in the wake of what they saw as the failure of West Indian emancipation. For a study of these emigrants, see Caree Banton, "'More Auspicious Shores': Post-Emancipation Barbadian Emigrants in Pursuit of Freedom, Citizenship and Nationhood in Liberia, 1834–1912" (Ph.D. diss., Vanderbilt University, 2013).

29. *Colonial Standard*, n.d., in Harrison to Marcy, Kingston, June 21, 1855, Despatches, vol. 16; Falmouth *Post*, June 19, 1855; Kingston *Morning Journal*, April 27, 1853; *Colonial Standard and Jamaica Dispatch*, April 26, 1853. My thanks to Shani Roper, former assistant curator at the Institute of Jamaica, for providing copies of these newspapers.

30. See undated newspaper reports of the inquiry in Harrison to Marcy, Kingston, May 24, July 12, 17, 1855, Despatches, vols. 16 and 17.

31. Henry Barkley to Harrison, King's House, July 12, 1855, and Harrison to Barkley, Kingston, July 19, 1855, both in Harrison to Marcy, Kingston, July 19, 1855, Harrison to Marcy, Kingston, July 26, 30, 1855, April 26, 1853, Despatches, vol. 17; Barkley to Lord Russell, King's House, July 25, 1855, CO 137/327, Colonial Office Document, National Archives, London.

32. Robin W. Winks, *The Blacks in Canada: A History* (New Haven, 1971), 174–75; Fred Landon, "The Anderson Fugitive Case," *Journal of Negro History* 7, no. 3 (July 1922): 233–42. See also Patrick Brode, *The Odyssey of John Anderson* (Toronto, 1989), for a biography of Anderson.

33. Kingston *Morning Journal*, April 27, 1853; *National Anti-Slavery Standard*, May 28, 1853; Falmouth *Post*, June 15, 1855.

CHAPTER 2

1. For a study of the history of the black communities in five towns—York, Columbia, Lancaster, West Chester, and Gettysburg—see Carl Douglas Oblinger, "New Freedoms, Old Miseries: The Emergence and Disruption of Black Communities in Southeastern Pennsylvania, 1780–1860," (Ph.D., diss., Lehigh University, 1988), 78–84; William C. Kashatus, *Just over the Line: Chester County and the Underground Railroad* (University Park, Pa., 2001), 57; James W. C. Pennington, *The Fugitive Blacksmith; or Events in the History of J.W.C. Pennington, Pastor of a Presbyterian Church, New York, Formerly a Slave in the State of Maryland, United States,* in Arna Bontemps, ed., *Great Slave Narratives* (Boston, 1969); William Craft, *Running a Thousand Miles for Freedom* (1860; repr., New York, 1969); Todd Mealy, *Biography of an Antislavery City: Antislavery Advocates, Abolitionists, and Underground Railroad Activists in Harrisburg, PA* (Baltimore, 2007), 33, 37; Gerald G. Eggert, "'Two Steps Forward, A Step-and-a-Half Back': Harrisburg's African American Community in the Nineteenth Century," *Pennsylvania History* 58, no. 1 (January 1991): 1.

2. *Pennsylvania Freeman,* August 29, 1850. On Taylor and Page, see both the 1850 Population Census and Slave Schedules for Clarke County, Va.; for Rawn, McKinney, and Pearson, see Mealy, *Biography of an Antislavery City,* 51, 132, and Michael Barton's introduction to the website "The Rawn Journals, 1830–1865," http://www.rawnjournals.com/about; for Jones and Thompson, see the 1850 and 1860 Population Census, Dauphin County, Pa., and Mary D. Houts, "Black Harrisburg's Resistance to Slavery," *Pennsylvania Heritage* 4, no. 1 (December 1977): 12.

3. Harrisburg *Telegraph,* August 28, 1850; Lancaster *Examiner & Herald,* August 28, 1850. The Richmond *Whig,* September 6, 1850, dismissed Pearson's reasoning and decision as "frivolous," resting as it did on a "dishonest distinction." An accompanying letter to the editor insisted that the governor of Virginia should demand the fugitives' return but doubted that he would since he would be fearful of being labeled a disunionist.

4. Harrisburg *Telegraph,* August 28, 1850; Lancaster *Examiner & Herald,* August 28, 1850; Gerald G. Eggert, "The Impact of the Fugitive Slave Law on Harrisburg: A Case Study," *Pennsylvania Magazine of History and Biography* 109 (October 1985): 540–43; Houts, "Black Harrisburg's Resistance to Slavery," 13; Dauphin County Clerk of Court, Quarter Session Docket Book 9, April 1855, p. 86, Dauphin County Courthouse, Harrisburg, Pa.

5. Eggert, "The Impact of the Fugitive Slave Law on Harrisburg," 545; Lebanon *Advertiser,* April 23, 1851.

6. Richard McAllister to John K. Kane, Harrisburg, n.d., RG 217, Settled Miscellaneous Treasury Accounts, September 6, 1790–September 29, 1894, National Archives, Washington, D.C. (hereafter cited as Selected Miscellaneous Treasury Accounts); Harrisburg *Telegraph,* October 9, 1850. The *Pennsylvania Freeman,* October 31, 1850, dismissed the posse as "kidnappers' pimps" and in the November 13, 1850,

issue wondered if it was legal to use a constabulary force for such purposes; Rawn Diary, Rawn Collection, MG 062, Diaries, Dauphin County Historical Society, Harrisburg, Pa. (hereafter cited as Rawn Diary).

7. Rawn Diary, November 22, 1850; *Pennsylvania Freeman*, December 12, 1850; Eggert, "The Impact of the Fugitive Slave Law on Harrisburg," 545. One Virginia newspaper estimated that it cost Taylor close to $1,400 to recapture his slaves, a price at least as high as the value of the slaves. *Southern Argus*, December 14, 1850.

8. Harrisburg *Union*, n.d., in Lebanon *Advertiser*, January 29, 1851; *Pennsylvania Telegraph*, January 25, 1851; McAllister to Kane, Harrisburg, January 30, 1851, Settled Miscellaneous Treasury Accounts.

9. Columbia *Spy*, April 26, 1851; Lancaster *Examiner & Herald*, April 30, 1851; Harrisburg *Daily American*, April 23, 1851; *Pennsylvania Freeman*, May 1, 1851; Rawn Diary, April 22, 1851; Eggert, "The Impact of the Fugitive Slave Law on Harrisburg," 546–47.

10. Harrisburg *Key Stone*, August 12, 1851; *Whig State Journal*, August 12, 1851; *Pennsylvania Freeman*, August 21, 1851; McAllister to Kane, Harrisburg, October 10, 1851, McAllister to Kane, Harrisburg, n.d., Settled Miscellaneous Treasury Accounts.

11. *Pennsylvania Freeman*, October 2, 1851; *Whig State Journal*, September 30, 1851; Harrisburg *Telegraph*, October 15, 1851; 1850 Population Census and Slave Schedule, Montgomery County, Md.

12. Harrisburg *Telegraph*, October 15, 1851.

13. Eggert, "The Impact of the Fugitive Slave Law on Harrisburg," 549; McAllister to Kane, Harrisburg, October 1, 1851, McAllister to E. C. Seaman, Harrisburg, October 19, 1851, Settled Miscellaneous Treasury Accounts; see also RG 39, Records of the Bureau of Accounts, Appropriation Ledger for the Treasury and Other Departments, 1807–1945, National Archives, Washington, D.C.

14. Harrisburg *Telegraph*, October 15, 1851; Eggert, "Impact of the Fugitive Slave Law on Harrisburg," 549–50.

15. McAllister to E. C. Seaman, Harrisburg, October 19, 1851, Settled Miscellaneous Treasury Accounts.

16. McAllister to Kane, Harrisburg, n.d., Solomon Snyder and Michael Shaffer to McAllister, Harrisburg, January 29, 1851, McAllister to Elisha Whittlesey, Harrisburg, February 1, 11, 1851, John Ashmead to Whittlesey, Philadelphia, February 7, 1851, Edward King to Dear Sir, Philadelphia, February 7, 1851, A. W. Loomis to Whittlesey, Pittsburgh, February 8, 11, 1851, Whittlesey to Thomas Smith, Washington, D.C., March 5, 1851, McAllister to E. C. Seaman, Harrisburg, October 19, 1851, McAllister to Kane, Harrisburg, June 9, 1862, Kane to McAllister, Philadelphia, July 5, 1852, Settled Miscellaneous Treasury Accounts. See also remittances from the Treasury Department, First Auditor's Office, March 8 and 10, 1851, to McAllister, Settled Miscellaneous Treasury Accounts.

17. Richmond *Dispatch*, May 3, 4, 5, 1852; West Chester *Village Record*, May 4,

1852; Lancaster *Examiner & Herald*, May 5, 12, 1852; *Pennsylvania Telegraph*, May 5, 1852; *Whig State Journal*, May 6, 13, 1852; Baltimore *Sun*, January 29, 1853; New York *Tribune*, May 4, 8, 1852; *Pennsylvania Freeman*, May 13, 27, 1852; *Frederick Douglass' Paper*, May 13, 1852; *National Anti-Slavery Standard*, May 6, 1852.

18. Lancaster *Examiner & Herald*, n.d., in West Chester *Village Record*, June 1, 1852, February 8, 1853.

19. *Pennsylvania Freeman*, May 13, 1852; Eggert, "The Impact of the Fugitive Slave Law on Harrisburg," 550–51.

20. *Pennsylvania Freeman*, June 3, 1852.

21. *Whig State Journal*, May 27, 1852; McAllister to Kane, Harrisburg, n.d., and June 9, 1852, Kane to McAllister, Philadelphia, July 5, 1852, Settled Miscellaneous Treasury Accounts; John Blassingame, *Slave Testimony: Two Centuries of Letters, Speeches, Interviews, and Autobiographies* (Baton Rouge, 1977), 95–96; Eggert, "The Impact of the Fugitive Slave Law on Harrisburg," 552–53.

22. Eggert, "The Impact of the Fugitive Slave Law on Harrisburg," 566; Harrisburg *Telegraph*, October 15, 1851, May 26, 1852; Rawn Diary, November 16, 1850; *Pennsylvania Freeman*, October 31, 1850, May 1, 1851; *Whig State Journal*, August 12, 1851; for earlier examples of organizations formed to prevent returns, see Edward R. Turner, "The Underground Railroad in Pennsylvania," *Pennsylvania Magazine of History and Biography* 36, no. 3 (1912): 315.

23. Eggert, "The Impact of the Fugitive Slave Law on Harrisburg," 562–63; *Pennsylvania Freeman*, March 24, 1853; New York *Tribune*, February 26, 1855.

24. *Anti-Slavery Bugle*, July 22, 1854; *Pennsylvanian*, February 1, 1853; Eggert, "The Impact of the Fugitive Slave Law on Harrisburg," 566–67; Mealy, *Biography of an Antislavery City*, 153–54.

25. *Pennsylvania Freeman*, January 30, 1852; Philadelphia *Cummins Evening Bulletin*, February 5, 1852; Washington *Daily Union*, January 16, March 23, June 27, July 24, October 11, 1851; *Whig State Journal*, August 12, 1851; *National Era*, July 3, 1851; W. W. Griest, ed., *Pennsylvania Archives*, vol. 7, *Papers of the Governors* (Harrisburg, 1902), 491–96, 520.

26. *Whig State Journal*, January 13, 1853; New York *Tribune*, January 16, 1852, January 31, February 1, 1856; Harrisburg *Semi-Weekly Telegraph*, May 12, 1856; Harrisburg *Telegraph*, February 20, 1857.

27. Kashatus, *Just over the Line*, 29–32.

28. *Pennsylvania Freeman*, February 20, 1851, April 20, 1854; Lancaster *Examiner & Herald*, June 18, 1856; M. G. Brubaker, "The Underground Railroad," *Lancaster County Historical Journal* 15, no. 4 (April 1911): 117. Another example of kidnapping in which the Gap Gang was involved, this time in Lancaster, is the case of John Williams in January 1851. See Lancaster *Union*, n.d., in New York *Tribune*, January 24, 1851; *Pennsylvania Freeman*, January 23, 1851; Lancaster *Examiner & Herald*, January 22, 1851; *Liberator*, January 31, 1851.

29. West Chester *Village Record*, January 13, February 10, 1852, January 18, 1853; Lancaster *Examiner & Herald*, December 31, 1851; Columbia *Spy*, January 3, 1852; *Cecil Whig*, December 27, 1851 (my thanks to Milt Diggins for this reference and for information on McCreary); *Pennsylvania Freeman*, January 22, 1852; Ralph Clayton, *Cash for Blood: The Baltimore to New Orleans Domestic Slave Trade* (Bowie, Md., 2002), 114.

30. West Chester *Village Record*, July 20, 1852, February 1, 1853; New York *Tribune*, January 22, 1853; *Pennsylvania Freeman*, January 20, 1853; *National Era*, August 5, 1852; *Liberator*, August 6, 1852.

31. West Chester *Village Record*, January 13, February 10, 1852; New York *Tribune*, January 22, 1853; Philadelphia *Cummins Evening Bulletin*, January 21, 1852.

32. West Chester *Village Record*, January 13, 20, 1852; *Pennsylvania Freeman*, January 8, 22, 29, 1852; Richmond *Dispatch*, January 31, 1852.

33. West Chester *Village Record*, January 13, 20, 27, February 10, 1852, January 25, 1853; Philadelphia *Cummins Evening Bulletin*, January 21, 1852; *Pennsylvania Freeman*, January 22, February 12, 1852; *National Era*, January 15, 1852; Lancaster *Examiner & Herald*, January 19, 1853.

34. West Chester *Village Record*, February 3, 10, April 15, 1852, January 11, 18, 20, 1853; *National Era*, January 15, April 24, 1852.

35. *Pennsylvania Freeman*, February 5, 1852; West Chester *Village Record*, February 24, April 15, 1852; *National Era*, April 24, 1852.

36. *Pennsylvanian Freeman*, January 20, March 3, 1853; West Chester *Village Record*, January 25, 1853.

37. West Chester *Register & Examiner*, n.d., in *Pennsylvania Freeman*, March 10, 1853.

38. *Pennsylvania Freeman*, June 30, 1852, January 20, 1853; West Chester *Village Record*, August 8, September 9, 1854. According to Milt Diggins, Lowe had also refused to extradite McCreary for one of two kidnappings in 1849. Correspondence with Milt Diggins, July 16, 2010.

39. Complaint of Fleming Hawkins, 1851 to 1853, Quarter Sessions Docket, Lancaster County Historical Society, Lancaster, Pa; *Whig State Journal*, May 19, 1853; *Daily Inland*, n.d., in Pittsburgh *Gazette*, May 25, 1853; *Anti-Slavery Bugle*, June 18, 1853.

40. Harrisburg *Telegraph & Journal*, March 10, 1855; New York *Tribune*, February 26, 1855; *Liberator*, March 16, 1855; Dauphin County Clerk of Courts, Quarter Session Docket Book 9, RG 47, County Records, Dauphin County Quarter Session, Oyer & Terminer Papers, True Bills, April/May 1855, Dauphin County Courthouse, Harrisburg, Pa.

41. Harrisburg *Telegraph*, February 28, March 2, 1857; RG 47, County Records, Dauphin County Quarter Session, Oyer & Terminer Papers, April 1857, Dauphin County Courthouse, Harrisburg, Pa.

42. S. S. Rutherford, "The Underground Railroad," *Publications of the Historical Society of Dauphin County* (1928): 7; Eggert, "The Impact of the Fugitive Slave Law on Harrisburg," 563, 566; Lancaster *Examiner & Herald*, December 8, 1852, January 26, 1853; New York *Tribune*, January 25, 1853; *Commonwealth v. John Anderson*, January session, 1853, Lancaster Historical Society, Lancaster, Pa. For other cases of black kidnappers, see Lancaster *Examiner & Herald*, June 4, 1856, July 22, 1857; Harrisburg *Telegraph*, July 21, 1857, Kashatus, *Just over the Line*, 31, and Marianne H. Russo and Paul A. Russo, *Hensonville, a Community at the Crossroads: The Story of a Nineteenth-Century African-American Village* (Selinsgrove, Pa., 2005), 79. The Russos argue there is no evidence that George Walls, a free black and an agent of the UGRR in Oxford, ever betrayed fugitives to catchers. They suggest that the rumor of Walls's collusion resulted possibly from the jealousy of "less prosperous black neighbors [who] secretly resented, rather than admired, his wealth."

43. West Chester *Village Record*, March 17, 1860; Harrisburg *Telegraph*, January 5, 1858. Early in the decade, during the inquiry into the killing of Smith in Columbia, Richard McAllister used his contacts with the two Maryland commissioners to win the release of John Johnson, a Harrisburg youth who had been caught in Maryland without a pass and bound out until he was twenty-one. Johnson's mother went door to door raising the $100 demanded for Johnson's release. He was finally returned in midsummer 1852 and delivered to his mother by McAllister. Many hoped his return would improve relations between Maryland and Pennsylvania. McAllister must have also calculated that his involvement would take the edge off his reputation as a callous commissioner. Lancaster *Examiner & Herald*, June 9, 1852; Baltimore *Sun*, June 4, 1852; Eggert, "The Impact of the Fugitive Slave Law on Harrisburg," 552.

44. *Pennsylvania Freeman*, November 18, 1852; Harrisburg *Morning Herald*, June 15, 1854. For similar "stampedes," see Kashatus, *Just over the Line*, 16.

45. Mealy, *Biography of an Antislavery City*, 71, 161, 165; William Still, *The Underground Railroad* (1872; repr., Chicago, 1970), 24–25; Harrisburg *Telegraph*, October 31, November 14, December 20, 1859, January 20, March 29, 1860; Pittsburgh *Gazette*, November 24, 1859; Kashatus, *Just over the Line*, 57–60.

46. For initial details of both cases, see Harrisburg *Telegraph*, April 2, 4, 1859; Philadelphia *Public Ledger*, March 27, 1860.

47. Harrisburg *Borough Times*, February 10, 15, 23, 24, 28, March 14, 1853. For a look at Chester's life in Liberia, see R. J. M. Blackett, *Thomas Morris Chester: Black Civil War Correspondent* (Baton Rouge, 1979).

48. Harrisburg *Telegraph*, July 28, August 10, 1857, December 19, 1859.

CHAPTER 3

1. Nashville *Gazette*, April 17, 27, August 17, 1860; Nashville *Post*, April 17, 1860; Nashville *Republican Banner*, April 17, 20, 26, 1860; Louisville *Courier*, April 16, 1860;

Seymour *Times*, April 19, 1860; Minutes, April 1860–December 1861, Division First, Davidson County Criminal Court, Nashville City Archives, Nashville, Tenn. James appears in the city jail in the 1860 Federal Census, Davidson County, Tenn.

2. Hannibal *Messenger*, December 8, 17, 20, 1853; *State of Missouri v Francis Moss*, box 45, folder 57, Circuit Court Case File, Missouri State Register of Inmates Received, Missouri State Library and Archives, Jefferson City. The Rowes' letter can be found in Office of the Secretary of State, Pardon Papers, 1837–1909, box 11, folder 29, RG 5, Missouri State Library and Archives, Jefferson City.

3. Easton *Star*, August 10, 1858; Secretary of State Pardon Records, 1845–1865, and Governor (Miscellaneous Papers), 1856, 1862–1865, both in Maryland State Archives, Annapolis; Kate Clifford Larson, *Bound for the Promised Land: Harriet Tubman, Portrait of an American Hero* (New York, 2004), 150.

4. Indiana *Free Democrat*, July 6, 1854; Thomas Brown, *Brown's Three Years in the Kentucky Prisons, From May 30, 1854, to May 18, 1857* (Indianapolis, 1857), in Paul Finkleman, ed., *Slave Rebels, Abolitionists and Southern Courts: The Pamphlet Literature*, series 4, vol. 2 (New York, 1988), 603–4, 619; Union County Circuit Court Case Files, box 80, bundle 392, Kentucky State Archives, Frankfort; Ann Hegedorn, *Beyond the River: The Untold Story of the Heroes of the Underground Railroad* (New York, 2002), 255–56; J. Blaine Hudson, *Fugitive Slaves and the Underground Railroad in the Kentucky Borderland* (Jefferson, N.C., 2002), 70, 84.

5. Richmond *Enquirer*, February 13, 1857; Louisville *Journal*, November 18, 1851; Louisville *Courier*, November 17, 18, 1851; *Liberator*, December 12, 1851, January 23, March 12, 1852; for Webster's involvement, see Randolph Paul Runyon, *Delia Webster and the Underground Railroad* (Lexington, Ky., 1996), chap. 6.

6. Nashville *Republican Banner*, April 11, 1857; Charles A. Sherrill, *Tennessee Convicts: Early Records of the State Penitentiary*, vol. 2, *1850–1870* (Mt. Juliet, Tenn., 2002), 274. See "Reports of the Agent and Keeper of the Tennessee Penitentiary for the Two Years Ending September 30, 1857," in Appendix to the Senate and House Journals, Tennessee, 1857–58, and *State of Tennessee v James Peck*, State Supreme Court Cases, Middle Tennessee, MT 259, both in Tennessee State Library and Archives, Nashville.

7. Easton *Gazette*, August 28, 1858; Richard Albert Blondo, "Samuel Green: A Black Life in Antebellum Maryland," (M.A. thesis, University of Maryland, 1988), 15–17; Larson, *Bound for the Promised Land*, 141–43.

8. Louisville *Journal*, April 6, 1855; Louisville *Courier*, April 6, 1855; Pamela A. Peters, *The Underground Railroad in Floyd County, Indiana* (Jefferson, N.C., 2001), 123.

9. West Chester *Village Record*, February 1, 1852; New York *Times*, January 27, 1853; Pittsburgh *Gazette*, January 29, 1853; *Anti-Slavery Bugle*, February 5, 1853; *Pennsylvania Freeman*, February 3, 1853. On Mayo, see Byron A. Lee, *Naval Warrior: The Life of Commodore Isaac Mayo* (Linthicum, Md., 2002).

10. Louisville *Journal*, May 9, 1860, August 14, 16, 17, 18, 1858; Louisville *Courier*,

May 9, 10, 1860, August 18, 20, 1858; Register of Prisoners, 1855–1861, Kentucky State Archives, Frankfort; Hudson, *Fugitive Slaves and the Underground Railroad in the Kentucky Borderland*, 90.

11. Louisville *Courier*, January 11, 1858; *Pennsylvania Freeman*, January 12, 1854.

12. Richmond *Enquirer*, June 15, 1855; *Southern Argus*, June 12, 19, 1855; Ira Berlin et al., eds., *Remembering Slavery: African Americans Talk about Their Personal Experiences in Slavery and Emancipation* (New York, 1994), 66–70.

13. Baltimore *Sun*, April 24, 1854; Journal C of Station 2 of the UGRR, 1852–1857, BAP, reel 7, 13387–88.

14. Hagerstown *Herald & Torch*, August 11, 18, 1852, May 28, June 4, 1856; Baltimore *Sun*, August 14, 1852; Harrisburg *Telegraph*, August 18, 1855.

15. Journal C of Station 2 of the UGRR, 1852–1857, BAP, reel 7, 13532–39, 13542–43.

16. Hagerstown *Herald of Freedom & Torch*, October 6, 1858.

17. James Rudd's Account Book, 1830–1860, James Rudd Papers, Filson Historical Society, Louisville, Ky. Thanks to P. Bogart, formerly of the Filson Historical Society library, for bringing this to my attention. Like James Armstrong, a slave named Davy escaped multiple times from Springfield, Tennessee, beginning in the summer of 1854. During one of these escapes he got as far as Indiana. At that point his owner decided to sell him. See John F. Baker Jr., *The Washingtons of Wessyngton Plantation: Stories of My Family's Journey to Freedom* (New York, 2009), 168–71.

18. Hagerstown *Herald & Torch*, October 11, 1854.

19. *Southern Argus*, April 20, August 22, 1854.

20. See Louisville *Courier*, October 25, December 24, 1853, February 20, July 1, 1854, for the ways the system functioned.

21. Ripley *Bee*, May 17, 1851; Louisville *Journal*, May 5, 1851, September 11, 1852; Louisville *Courier*, October 4, 1852; Sherman W. Savage, "The Contest Over Slavery Between Illinois and Missouri," *Journal of Negro History* 28, no. 3 (July 1943): 324; Oleta Prisloo, "The Case of 'The Dyed-in-the-Wool Abolitionists' in Mark Twain's Country, Marion County, Missouri: An Examination of a Slaveholding Community's Response to Radical Abolitionism in the 1830s and 1840s" (Ph.D. diss., University of Missouri–Columbia, 2003), 316; Slavery–Slave Patrol Preamble, 1856, box 2, folder 26, Walton Collection, Tennessee State Library and Archives, Nashville.

22. Robert Ryland, "Reminiscences of the First African Church, Richmond, VA.," *American Baptist Memorial* 14 (November 1855): 323; Gregg D. Kimball, *American City, Southern Place: A Cultural History of Antebellum Richmond* (Athens, Ga., 2000), 148–49; Richmond *Enquirer*, September 3, 1853.

23. Hagerstown *Herald of Freedom & Torch*, October 6, 1858; *Southern Argus*, April 20, 1854.

24. See John Hope Franklin and Loren Schweninger, *Runaway Slaves: Rebels on the Plantation* (New York, 1999), for an exploration of these issues.

25. Chicago *Tribune*, January 25, 1855.

26. *Acts of the General Assembly: Passed in 1855,* (Richmond, 1856), 28–41.

27. Staunton *Free American,* January 3, 1856. James M. Prichard discusses the ways the court system worked to limit the activities of slavery's opponents in an unpublished essay, "Into the Fiery Furnace: Anti-Slavery Prisoners in the Kentucky State Penitentiary 1844–1870."

28. "Report of the Select Committee," *Virginia General Assembly, House of Delegates, 1848–1849* (Richmond, 1848–1849), 10; Richmond *Enquirer,* July 12, 1855.

29. Hagerstown *Herald of Freedom & Torch,* December 21, 1853; Richmond *Dispatch,* October 24, 1853.

30. Richmond *Dispatch,* April 26, 1853.

31. Curtis Jacobs Diary, Maryland Historical Society, Baltimore.

32. *Debates and Proceedings of the Maryland Reform Convention to Revise the State Constitution,* vol. 2 (Annapolis, 1851), 220–23. By the end of the decade, a number of southern states, including Tennessee and Arkansas, would adopt laws calling for the expulsion of free blacks.

33. See Barbara J. Fields, *Slavery and Freedom on the Middle Ground: Maryland during the Nineteenth Century* (New Haven, 1985), for a discussion of these developments.

34. Easton *Gazette,* August 28, 1858, September 18, 25, October 30, November 13, 1858; Baltimore *Sun,* November 6, 1858.

35. Easton *Gazette,* December 11, 1858; Baltimore *Sun,* June 9, 10, 1859; Curtis W. Jacobs, *The Free Negro Question* (Baltimore, 1859), 5–6, 14–15, and *Speech of Col. Curtis W. Jacobs on the Free Colored Population of Maryland Delivered in the House of Delegates, on the 17th of February, 1860* (Annapolis, 1860), 10. On Fitzhugh's argument, see George Fitzhugh, *Cannibals All! Or Slaves Without Masters* (1856; repr., Cambridge, Mass., 1973).

36. Frederick *Herald,* February 7, 1860; Easton *Gazette,* November 10, 1860.

CONCLUSION

1. For coverage of the case, see Cincinnati *Gazette,* May 8, 17, 18, 19, 1858; Cincinnati *Commercial,* May 8, 9, 15, 24, 1858; *Liberator,* July 2, 1858.

2. Franklin A. Wilmot, *Disclosures and Confessions of Frank A. Wilmot, the Slave Thief and Negro Runner* (Philadelphia, 1860), 15, 19, 20–21, 25–26, 30, 33, 35–36.

3. Harrisburg *Union & Patriot,* November 23, 1859.

4. John Blassingame, *Slave Testimony: Two Centuries of Letters, Speeches, Interviews, and Autobiographies* (Baton Rouge, 1977), 114.

5. E. P. Thompson, *Customs in Common* (New York, 1991), 212.

6. Charles Wise, P. Williamson, and William Still to respected Friends, Philadelphia, August 30, 1854, Pennsylvania Abolition Society Papers, Pennsylvania Historical Society, Philadelphia.

7. Philadelphia *Cummins Evening Bulletin*, April 5, 6, 7, 1859; Philadelphia *Public Ledger*, April 5, 1859; Harrisburg *Telegraph*, April 2, 4, 6, 7, 1859.

8. Harrisburg *Telegraph*, April 2, 1859; Philadelphia *Cummins Evening Bulletin*, April 9, 1859.

9. Harrisburg *Telegraph*, April 7, 9, 1859.

10. Philadelphia *Cummins Evening Bulletin*, April 6, 1859.

11. Harrisburg *Telegraph*, September 6, 1897.

Index